VGM Professional Careers Series

FINANCE

TRUDY RING

THIRD EDITION

VGM Career Books

New York   Chicago   San Francisco   Lisbon   London   Madrid   Mexico City
Milan   New Delhi   San Juan   Seoul   Singapore   Sydney   Toronto

The **McGraw·Hill** Companies

Library of Congress Cataloging-in-Publication Data

Ring, Trudy.
 Careers in finance/Trudy Ring.—3rd ed.
  p. cm.—(VGM professional careers series)
  ISBN 0-07-143736-3
 1. Finance—Vocational guidance. 2. Banks and banking—Vocational
guidance. I. Title. II. Series.
  HG173.R55 2004
  332'.023'73—dc22

                                      2004004130

      4 5 6 7 8 9 0   DSH/DSH   0 1 0 9 8 7 6

ISBN 0-07-143736-3

Interior design by Robert S. Tinnon

McGraw-Hill books are available at special quantity discounts to use as premiums and sales promotions, or for use in corporate training programs. For more information, please write to the Director of Special Sales, Professional Publishing, McGraw-Hill, Two Penn Plaza, New York, NY 10121-2298. Or contact your local bookstore.

This book is printed on acid-free paper.

CONTENTS

ACKNOWLEDGMENTS

The author wishes to thank all of those financial service professionals and others who shared their knowledge and insights during the preparation of this book. Special appreciation goes to the communications staffs of the many financial services organizations cited in the book.

Last, thanks to my friends and family for their moral support that has proven so valuable in my writing career and in all aspects of my life.

The editors extend their appreciation to Mark Rowh, a professional writer and author of a number of career books, for his effort in revising and updating this edition.

FOREWORD

"**M**oney makes the world go around." So sang the emcee in the musical *Cabaret*, and he was right. No matter what type of business you're in, profit or nonprofit, manufacturing or service, money management is the key to long-term success. In recent years, firms in the financial services industry have experienced a dramatic transformation in the way they do business. Computer technology has enabled companies to be more efficient, so there is less emphasis on number crunching and a greater focus on analytical skills. The globalization of financial markets has increased the challenges facing financial professionals and, at the same time, created the opportunity to expand careers across international borders. Innovative financial products are changing the very nature of the financial services industry, providing an opportunity for young, creative thinkers to succeed in a new era.

As this book demonstrates in great detail, financial careers span the gamut of human endeavor. Hospitals need experienced financial officers to make sure money is available to buy the latest equipment and medicines, maintain an efficient facility, and hire quality personnel to treat the sick. Universities need sophisticated money management to maintain and grow their campuses, attract and keep professors, enrich programs for their students, and provide financial aid to qualified applicants. And governments need financial wizards of unending creativity and perseverance to help them deal with the growing monetary crises they have experienced during the past several years of recession and global political turmoil.

Financial services professionals are the people who, in a very direct way, deliver the capital and financial management critical to all business. As president of the Financial Women's Association of New York, I've had the opportunity to see the tremendous scope of financial services. All types of people with enormous varieties of skills and talents find successful careers in finance.

Because you're reading this, you're undoubtedly considering such a career. I encourage you to read on and learn about the new and exciting options careers in finance offer. This book will help you decide if one of them is for you. If so, I encourage you to work hard to pursue your choice. Good luck!

MINA KNOLL
Past President,
Financial Women's Association of New York

C H A P T E R

FINANCIAL SERVICES: AN INTRODUCTION

A popular stereotype often comes to mind when we think of a financial services practitioner: the Wall Street tycoon, clad in a pinstriped suit, carrying an expensive leather briefcase, armed with an MBA degree from a prestigious school, and practicing a profession that has plenty of glamour and excitement as well as an aura of greed and obsessive self-interest. Another popular stereotype is that of the brilliant but socially awkward number cruncher: unkempt appearance, ever-present calculator, and eyes glazed over from staring at a computer screen.

In reality, the field of financial services and the people who work in it are far more diverse than these or other pervasive images would lead us to believe. It is a field that offers a wide range of career opportunities to many people who do not fit any of the stereotypes of financial wizards. People employed in finance affect almost every aspect of business—indeed, life itself—because money still does make the world go around.

Consider the impact these financial practitioners have made. Corporate finance officers help their companies raise capital that often funds new plants or new products, resulting in new jobs. Public finance professionals raise money to build roads, bridges, schools, and hospitals. Lending officers at banks, savings and loans, and credit unions help their customers finance homes or college educations. Portfolio managers invest the retirement savings of millions of people.

Those who pursue careers in finance in the coming years will find that their activities are increasingly global in nature. Economic events in the United States will affect the rest of the world, and vice versa. Technology will make cross-border financing and investing easier and more common than they have ever been. Stock markets and other capitalist institutions will continue to grow in developing nations and former Communist countries. It will be an exciting time to be involved in the wide variety of careers available in financial services.

CAREER OPTIONS

We will look in this book at the various careers available in finance, the duties involved, the skills and training required, and the outlook for growth or contraction in financial services employment. The career fields, to be explored in detail in the following chapters, fall into several broad categories.

Corporate and Public Finance

People who work in corporate financial departments are involved in raising money through issue of stocks or bonds; investment of various corporate funds; collection of money owed to the company; and the disbursement of checks to employees, suppliers, and creditors. Workers in public finance offices handle borrowing, investing, collection, and disbursement for government entities, including cities, states, counties, and school districts. Colleges and universities, charitable foundations, and many nonprofit organizations employ finance and investment officers to handle duties similar to those in the corporate or public sectors.

Investment Banking

Corporate, public, and other financial officers often enlist the help of outside experts. Investment bankers help their clients create issues of stocks, bonds, or other types of securities; they also underwrite (insure) and help market those securities. In addition, investment bankers often advise clients on mergers, acquisitions, and other actions that have a financial impact.

Banks, S&Ls, and Credit Unions

Commercial banks, savings and loan (S&L) associations, and credit unions offer loans, savings and checking accounts, and other services to businesses, governmental bodies, and consumers.

Portfolio Management

Portfolio management professionals invest money for corporate and public pension funds, charitable foundations and educational endowments, and individuals. Some portfolio management firms are independently owned, either by their key employees or a group of public shareholders; some are subsidiaries of banks, insurance companies, or nonfinancial corporations. Some firms specialize in one type of investment—stocks, bonds, real estate, or venture capital; others offer a variety of choices. Some cater primarily to institutions—pension funds, foundations, and endowments. Others are popular with individuals, especially mutual fund companies, which pool the money of numerous clients for greater investment clout. Some individuals, however, turn to personal financial planners, who offer custom-tailored advice on investments, insurance, and other money matters.

Trading

Brokers and traders execute portfolio managers' orders to buy or sell stocks, bonds, or other securities, such as commodities, futures, and options. Brokerage firms generally are affiliated with investment banking firms. Brokers also may offer research on various securities or investment strategies. Security trades may be made through private arrangements between investors, but more often they happen on the many public stock and commodity exchanges around the world. These exchanges employ people to assure that trading goes smoothly, to develop new financial instruments, and to act as liaisons to the investment community.

THE JOB MARKET

The last few decades have been a tumultuous time for financial services. During the early and middle parts of the 1980s, the industry expanded rapidly, fueled by the booming stock market and the corporate mania for mergers and acquisitions. Toward the end of the 1980s, a retrenchment took place due to factors including the October 1987 stock market crash when the Dow plunged more than 500 points, the fear that companies had taken on excessive debt in the merger and acquisition frenzy, and the general economic slowdown around the world. The financial services job market experienced periods of both growth and decline in the 1990s and on into the present century. Some sectors have been far healthier than others. The overall field is quite large, however, and significant career opportunities are available for those with the right credentials.

Outlook on Investment Banking

Within investment banking, opportunities will be greatest for people who familiarize themselves with the most innovative and specialized financing products and who help clients learn to use them. Those who understand the latest finance innovations will likely have an edge in obtaining jobs in corporate treasury departments.

Commercial banks have undergone a great deal of change in recent years. An upside to this is that job opportunities may arise as some banks "clean house" and bring in new management teams. In times of transition, career opportunities will become available for some people, especially those who have prepared themselves by developing the proper qualifications.

Outlook on Investment Management

Investment management will offer good opportunities in the coming years. There is plenty of demand for firms that manage corporate and public pension funds even though the growth of pension assets has slowed in recent years. Growth is expected in mutual funds, which have become the most cost-effective way for individuals to invest their money, and which have been shrewdly marketed. Mutual funds have also been the vehicle for some pension assets.

Outlook on Trading

The brokerage business continues to hold promise, even though brokers must now compete with online trading opportunities and have been under pressure from clients to lower their fees on simple trades. Expansion can be expected in a number of markets—both in the United States and around the world—and there will be continued globalization of the financial markets in general. It may be a good idea to think about a career in an international post; working in another country requires flexibility, adaptability, and foreign language skills.

PROFILE OF A VALUABLE JOB APPLICANT

Most companies and nonprofit organizations that employ financial professionals have no shortage of job applicants. Faced with an abundance of potential employees, they can be highly selective, giving many applications only cursory consideration. And even when this is not the case, employers naturally seek the most highly qualified workers available. As a result, it only makes sense to "package" yourself to have as many attributes as possible that are valuable to a potential employer.

Skills and Characteristics

One way job seekers can become competitive in today's business world is to have an international orientation. Mathematical and analytical skills are important, too. Many finance professionals emphasize, however, that the technical aspects of the business often can be learned on the job. Liberal arts majors and others without an extensive mathematical background need not shy away from finance, provided they have some interest and aptitude. With so many aspects of the business being computerized, computer skills are considered to be of great importance.

Many companies are making individual ethics and integrity more of an issue than they have for some time. Possibly, this is in response to insider-trading and other recent financial scandals. Employers are also interested in workers' ability to build and maintain good relationships with their colleagues and clients. A lost client might be irreplaceable in today's financial climate.

Employers are placing renewed emphasis on communications skills as well. Lack of these skills is the biggest complaint that many companies have about the current crop of applicants. Employees should be able to stand before a group and make a presentation, and they need to have good writing skills.

Other things that companies like to see in applicants are realistic expectations—not presuming to advance to top management or make a six-figure salary overnight—and practical work experience, through internships, summer jobs, or relevant volunteer work.

A master's of business administration (MBA) degree can give applicants the edge for some jobs. In recent years, the MBA has become what some consider the key to the kingdom of success in financial services. Experts report, however, that this is not necessarily true in all cases. We'll look next at the debate about the value of an MBA. See Appendix C for a listing of selected universities and colleges that offer finance and banking courses.

THE MBA

In the last couple of decades, the MBA has acquired a definite mystique, as have the nation's top business schools. This may have been diminished somewhat by recent economic problems and a tough market for job seekers in many fields, but the MBA is still an attractive commodity in the financial world. In fact, a popular perception is that an MBA or equivalent degree is an absolute necessity for anyone who wants to rise to the top in financial services or any other aspect of commerce. In reality, though, whether an MBA is crucial to meeting one's career goals differs greatly from one individual to another and from one employer to another.

MBAs abound in certain segments of the financial services market, such as investment banks and large money-center commercial banks. They also are common in portfolio management firms and corporate financial departments. However, numerous people have become millionaires in commodity futures trading without having an MBA, and, in some cases, even without a bachelor's degree.

Getting an MBA from a top business school may make an employee more attractive to some employers, while having an MBA from a third-class institution may not substantially increase your chances for success. According to Duke University, which surveys graduates of top-tier business schools annually, starting salaries for 2003 MBA graduates averaged nearly $88,000.

Michael, a product manager for a major financial institution, says having an MBA from one of the nation's top business schools helped to advance his career. Michael worked in the insurance and reinsurance industries for five years before entering Northwestern's Kellogg Graduate School of Management, where he earned an MBA with a concentration in marketing, international business, and management. At that time, the job market was highly competitive because the economy was starting to weaken. Having a Kellogg MBA, however, increased his marketability. "The name alone opened a lot of doors," he says. Kellogg has a powerful alumni network, with many graduates in high-level corporate jobs. Although some of Michael's Kellogg education was not as helpful as he expected, other aspects of his MBA studies were relevant. The course work helped him learn how to think critically and make decisions. Knowing what he knows now, he says, he still would go for his MBA.

So, how do you decide if an MBA is necessary to your career? For one thing, you can find out if MBAs are common in the field in which you want to work. (Subsequent chapters in this book will provide some of that information.) Also, it is a good idea to ask your professors, placement personnel, and people who are employed in your desired area. Keep in mind that even in job categories where MBAs do not abound, an MBA can help give you an edge in an especially competitive market.

For those who decide to go for an MBA, there is the additional decision of whether to attend school full-time or part-time. Those who go full-time are definitely taking a risk by quitting their jobs. On the other hand, if someone has been out of work for a while, this may be a good time to go full-time to business school.

Michael, the product manager, says quitting work to go to school full-time was the right decision for him. "I felt I would not get the high-quality education I wanted with the distraction of a full-time job," he says. He also knew he did not want to stay at the company where he worked before going to Kellogg. So he used his savings and took out loans to go to school full-time.

Attending school on a part-time basis may work well for some people, especially if they want to stay with their current employer and the employer has a policy of paying for graduate study. People who go to school part-time may feel that a great load is lifted off their shoulders because their company paid for their degree.

It is usually a good idea to work for a few years after receiving a bachelor's degree before pursuing an MBA; three or four years is generally enough.

Michael says his work experience was valuable during his MBA study. He was able to draw parallels between his experience and topics that were being discussed in his classes. His previous employment also increased his self-confidence and encouraged him to speak up in class.

Business Schools

Naturally, in addition to the decisions about whether, how, and when to go for an MBA, a big question is where to go. Again, your professors, guidance and placement officers, and people who already have received their MBAs can provide information on which schools may suit your needs. Business publications are also an excellent source of background about business schools. Some of the top business schools in the nation are at the following universities and colleges: Northwestern, Harvard, Dartmouth, University of Pennsylvania, Cornell, University of Michigan, Stanford, Duke, University of Chicago, and Indiana University. Applications to these programs and others have soared, leading to keen competition for admission.

The MBA Alternative

In 1992, the Stuart School of Business at the Illinois Institute of Technology (IIT) in Chicago began offering a degree program that may become a popular alternative to MBA study. By offering a master of science degree in financial markets and trading, IIT has the world's first degree program in the study of modern capital markets.

Although most MBA programs have some courses on finance, IIT's program provides concentrated study designed specifically to meet the needs of financial institutions. It includes courses on the traditional markets, such as stocks, bonds, and currencies, as well as the newer ones, including options and futures.

Earning the degree will take a year and a half for full-time students and two years for those who attend part-time. All faculty members for the program are people who work in the financial services industry. It has an advisory board made up of representatives of numerous financial services companies and securities exchanges and is headed by the chairperson of the Chicago Corporation, an investment banking firm.

Other programs have also been developed in specialized areas related to finance. For example, the interdisciplinary master of science degree in financial engineering (MSFE) offered by Kent State University is designed for students with strong quantitative background with the goal of becoming risk management officers and/or traders. The program combines the strengths of strong quantitative skills from mathematics, including probability and numerical computing, joined with risk management skills and valuation skills from finance.

The University of California, Berkeley, is another institution offering a master's in financial engineering program through its Haas School of Business. Faculty members include not only those from Haas, but also professors from UCLA's Anderson School and the UC Irvine School of Management. Students in this program learn to employ theoretical finance and computer modeling skills to make pricing, hedging, trading, and portfolio management decisions. Courses and projects emphasize the practical applications of these skills.

Program graduates are prepared for careers in areas such as investment banking, corporate strategic planning, risk management, financial information systems management, portfolio management, and securities trading.

As another example, the Global Institute of Finance and Banking in New York City offers a master of science degree program as a collaborative initiative between the Global Institute of Finance and Banking and Mercy

College. Students in this program prepare for careers as financial services professionals in areas such as securities management.

COPING WITH A DIVERSE WORKFORCE

Professional and managerial jobs in financial services were once the exclusive domain of white males. That has slowly changed during the past few decades. Women and members of minority groups are no longer rare at gatherings of financial executives; many of them are either successful entrepreneurs or high-ranking officers of some of the largest firms in the industry. Although some traces of discrimination remain, it appears that many employers are making a concerted effort to assure a comfortable, equal opportunity workplace for an increasingly diverse workforce.

For instance, Goldman Sachs, one of the largest investment banking firms in the United States, formed a diversity committee to deal with issues of race and gender. One of the committee's first efforts was to expand its list of recruitment schools and to build strong relationships with the deans, placement directors, and students at these schools. Along these lines, Goldman developed close ties with predominantly African American schools such as Howard University, Florida A&M University, Morehouse College, and Spelman College. The committee also developed training courses aimed at heightening Goldman employees' awareness of and sensitivity to issues of diversity.

As a result of this work, Goldman began offering numerous benefits of interest to workers who are part of two-career couples or who have small children. These included flexible work arrangements, such as job sharing, flexible hours, and telecommuting (working at home while being linked to a Goldman office by phone, computer, and facsimile machine). Such arrangements allow employees to stay with the firm instead of leaving when a spouse takes a job in another city or when a child is born. This is not just good for the employee; it is advantageous for the company and makes good business sense. Knowledgeable and skilled people are retained and the time and expense of hiring and training replacements are avoided.

Another development was the creation of an emergency backup child-care center at Goldman's New York headquarters. The center was designed to give employees a place to take their children when normal child-care arrangements are disrupted—for instance, when the school is closed or when the usual care provider is ill.

Many other financial services companies have established programs to deal with a diverse workforce and to make the workplace friendlier to employees with family responsibilities. The question remains, however: How much have attitudes really changed? That inquiry brings varying responses.

Patricia's experience as a high-ranking member of the financial services industry is illustrative. She is president of a large firm that invests billions of dollars on behalf of pension funds, foundations, endowments, and other institutional clients. She says that the industry is not a particularly difficult environment for women and minorities. Finance, and especially its investment management component, allows for employees' performance to be gauged objectively. Whether one's efforts made or lost money, and how much they made or lost, is easily quantifiable. Because an employee's performance can be easily illustrated, employees tend to be judged on performance, not gender or race.

She also points out that many public pension funds and other potential investment clients have affirmative action guidelines in place for their investment management arrangements. They may set aside a portion of their business for small, entrepreneurial firms owned by women or minorities, or insist that larger firms providing investment management services have women or minorities represented in management positions. Some corporate and government entities have adopted similar guidelines for their investment banking, brokerage, or commercial banking relationships.

John, a successful African American entrepreneur, whose firm invests billions of dollars for a long list of clients, says he hasn't encountered racial barriers in the business. "Our customers have been very good to us," he says. "If there are some potential clients whose attitudes aren't good, there are plenty of others who are practically bending over backward to hire minority firms."

Being pioneers actually can be helpful to minorities and women. If they can identify a business in which their numbers are small, and make themselves a visible, important part of the organization, they may experience a swift rise to the top.

Some entrepreneurs point out that traditionally, investors have not routed money to female or minority venture capitalists. Minorities and women say that sometimes they have trouble obtaining access to established business networks, or even being taken seriously in the finance industry. In some cases, others may perceive that they have reached their positions for reasons other than merit. Some feel that the problem of prejudice must be attacked on a society-wide basis, beginning in childhood.

Out of these varying impressions, what is the bottom line for women and minorities considering careers in finance? Certainly, they should not let anything keep them from pursuing the jobs they desire. At the same time, employers, clients, and other business contacts who are not open to diversity should be encouraged to become more receptive—and those who already are should be commended.

ENTREPRENEURSHIP

Most people spend their lives working for someone else, and many of them are perfectly content to do so. For those who possess the necessary characteristics and are willing to take the risk, however, the financial services industry offers great opportunities for people who want to start their own firms.

Few people become entrepreneurs right out of school; experience helps when starting your own operation. Some have taken the entrepreneurial route quite young, though. John was only twenty-four years old when he started his own investment management firm. He had worked as a stockbroker for a large company for two years after receiving his bachelor's degree in economics. He founded his own company primarily because he had an investment philosophy that he believed in—and because he doubted another employer would give him a chance to try out his strategy.

A major problem for the new enterprise was developing a track record. In the investment business, potential clients generally like to see a firm's past achievements before entrusting it with significant amounts of capital. John dealt with this issue by being willing to take on small amounts of business initially—say, $100,000 out of a multimillion-dollar university endowment fund—with the hope that good performance would lead to increased commitments from clients. Happily for John, his firm produced positive results for its clients, and its base of business grew accordingly.

Another early problem for the new company was attracting high-quality employees for salaries less than the industry norm. John's solution was to promise his employees competitive pay when the firm grew larger and became profitable, the opportunity to own a portion of the firm, and a pleasant work environment.

Other factors necessary to entrepreneurial success, John says, include maintaining a high profile and being involved in all aspects of the business. To keep his name in front of the public, John publishes a newsletter that offers investment tips and stays active in the philanthropic community, serving on the boards of several charitable organizations. As for being involved in every aspect of the business, he says entrepreneurs need to understand not only the product or service they are offering, but how to sell it and how to run the company's day-to-day operations. "Just focusing on one aspect of the firm is probably where some entrepreneurs get in trouble," he says. "One of the most crucial things" he adds, "is to do what you say you're going to do. Keep your customers happy, and they'll tell other people."

Being an entrepreneur generally means working long hours—nine- to fifteen-hour days are common—and having little security because there is no guaranteed paycheck. There is, however, great satisfaction in having control over your own destiny.

Self-confidence is one of the most important traits an entrepreneur can possess. "People who lack confidence or who have trouble making decisions are doomed in this business," says Bill, a successful stock options trader.

Whether as entrepreneurs or as employees of large organizations, individuals going into financial services have an enormous variety of career options. We start looking at them in the next chapter.

CHAPTER

2

CORPORATE AND PUBLIC FINANCE DEPARTMENTS

Whether or not its main business focus is finance, every corporation employs a certain number of finance professionals. So does almost every governmental unit, educational institution, and nonprofit organization. Most of them offer entry-level jobs as well as advancement opportunities. Finance professionals employed by these organizations carry out such duties as borrowing, investing, collecting, and disbursing funds for the employer; conducting budget planning; performing financial support services; and providing overall financial management.

THE CORPORATE WORLD

In very small corporations, one person—the treasurer—may handle all of the financial duties. More commonly, however, a corporate finance department has multiple staff members, each with specific duties.

A medium- to large-sized corporation is likely to have a treasurer, a controller (sometimes called comptroller), and a risk manager, each with a staff of assistants and analysts, and all reporting to the chief financial officer.

Treasurer

The treasurer and his or her staff usually have responsibility for the company's capital-raising activities—the issuance of stocks and bonds. Stocks are securities that give the holder ownership of a portion of the company. Bonds are securities through which the company borrows money, promising to pay back the bondholder's initial investment—plus interest—over a given period of time.

Treasury staffers generally work with advisers from investment banking firms when developing stock or bond issues. The treasury staff is usually responsible for investor relations; that is, communicating with holders of the company's stocks or bonds.

Another activity handled by the treasury staff is investing. Many companies have several million dollars in retirement funds; good investments keep this money growing, so the firm will not have to struggle financially to meet its obligations to present and future retirees. Companies often delegate the actual investment of this money to a group of portfolio management firms; however, the treasury staff must monitor the investment results produced by these companies and decide when a firm should be replaced. Some corporations maintain their own treasury staffs to do the actual investment of a portion—or occasionally all—of their retirement funds. This is known as in-house investment management. A handful of nonfinancial corporations have begun to market their investment expertise to other companies and individuals.

Cash management—another treasury responsibility—involves investing as well.

Typically, these investments are more short term in nature than the investments made for retirement funds (for example, ninety-day Treasury bills rather than ten-year bonds). Corporate cash managers also have some capital-raising responsibilities, often through the issuance of short-term debt securities called commercial paper. Another aspect of cash management is setting up and maintaining arrangements with commercial banks to ensure the timely deposit of money owed to the company and payout of funds it owes.

Controller

A controller (or comptroller) is the key financial executive who controls, analyzes, and interprets the financial results and records of a company or an organization.

A treasurer, on the other hand, is responsible for the receipt, custody, and properly organized disbursement of an organization's or company's funds.

Some organizations also have a vice president of finance who has overall financial responsibility and reports to the chief executive officer—president or chair of the board—of the company.

A company may employ one or all of these financial officers or combine all three into one executive-level position with any of the above titles. This job description is confined to the usual duties of a controller in an organization that has a separate treasurer position.

The controller is responsible for designing a company's accounting system(s), preparing budgets and financial forecasts, performing internal audits of company operations and records, controlling company funds kept by the treasurer, establishing and administering tax policies and procedures, and preparing reports made to government agencies. Since an organization's financial operations involve accumulating, interpreting, and storing vast amounts of detailed information, a controller is very often in charge of the company's computerized data processing operation as well.

Controllers are employed throughout the United States and Canada. They work for government agencies, businesses, nonprofit organizations, hospitals, and other institutions of all sizes.

As with many top-level jobs, controllers often work long hours under great pressure. Peak workloads occur when tax reports and stockholders' reports are prepared.

Potential and Advancement

The career paths to the position of controller are varied. Cost analysis and accounting, budgeting, tax auditing, financial analysis, planning and programming, credit collections, systems and procedures, and data processing are all training grounds for executive-level financial positions.

Once the top-management level has been reached, the usual method of advancement for a controller is to transfer to a larger organization where the responsibilities are greater and more complex. Some advance by moving from a top financial position in a large organization to the chief executive post in a smaller one. About 30 percent of all chief executive officers come up through the financial area.

Risk Manager

The risk management staff is responsible for buying and maintaining corporate insurance. This includes insurance on the company's buildings and vehicles, liability insurance, and employee medical insurance. In a company with overseas facilities and/or markets, the risk manager may handle currency hedging—various investment strategies designed to guard against loss from exposure to foreign currencies. Handling corporate tax matters is another risk management duty.

Employee Qualifications and Characteristics

Entry-level employees generally perform a variety of analytical duties related to the treasurer's, controller's, or risk manager's functions. A bachelor's degree often sufficiently qualifies an individual for entry-level jobs in investing or cash management. For jobs in capital raising or budget analysis, companies tend to prefer MBAs. Important characteristics for corporate financial employees are that they be bright, ambitious, and hardworking.

In companies that are growing quickly, talented entry-level employees may be promoted to a supervisory position within eighteen to twenty-four months.

If company growth is slower, this may take three to four years. A company's head treasurer, controller, or risk manager generally has ten to twelve years of experience, and a chief financial officer—who oversees all financial functions of the company—usually has fifteen to twenty.

Salaries

The corporate financial sector can be a lucrative one, but salaries vary widely according to the size of the company and the industry in which its primary business lies. According to the U.S. Department of Labor, median annual earnings of financial managers were $67,020 in 2000. The middle 50 percent earned between $48,150 and $91,580. The lowest 10 percent had earnings of less than $36,050, while the top 10 percent earned over $131,120. Table 2.1 shows average salaries for financial managers in various industries in 2000.

Table 2.1 Salaries of Financial Managers

Security brokers and dealers	$112,140
Accounting, auditing, and bookkeeping	83,380
Computer and data processing services	79,850
Local government	59,000
Commercial banks	55,960

Source: U.S. Department of Labor

According to a 2001 survey by Robert Half International, a staffing services firm specializing in accounting and finance, directors of finance earned between $70,750 and $202,750, and corporate controllers earned between $53,500 and $150,250.

Details from the Association for Financial Professionals' thirteenth annual compensation survey are presented in Table 2.2. The earnings listed in the table represent total compensation, including bonuses and deferred compensation, for 2001. Financial officers' average total compensation was $122,170.

Large organizations often pay more than small ones, and salary levels also can depend on the type of industry and location. Many financial managers in private industry receive additional compensation through bonuses, which also vary substantially by size of firm. Deferred compensation in the form of stock options also is becoming more common.

Table 2.2 Average Earnings for Selected Financial Managers, 2001

Vice president of finance	$178,724
Treasurer	158,404
Assistant vice president–finance	128,272
Controller/comptroller	119,220
Director	110,704
Assistant treasurer	105,885
Assistant controller/comptroller	99,856
Manager	81,720
Cash manager	60,424

Source: Association for Financial Professionals

The Job Outlook

While there will be a continuing need for these types of financial professionals in the foreseeable future, demand at any one time depends on the overall state of the economy as well as localized conditions within any hiring organization. During economic downturns, for example, applicants for corporate finance jobs may have to work harder at finding jobs as many companies trim the ranks of their white-collar workers. At the same time, there is likely to be a niche for candidates with the right combination of qualifications, especially those with up-to-date knowledge of financial innovations.

THE PUBLIC SECTOR

The business world may be the primary employer of financial professionals, but it is not the only game in town. Government is also a big business, in a sense, and the affairs of governmental agencies include a variety of financial processes. The same is true of schools, colleges, hospitals, professional associations, and other nonprofit organizations. Budgets must be created and administered. Employees must be paid. Equipment and supplies must be purchased. These and other functions require the expertise of financial professionals.

Government

Finance is essential to the operation of government at every level—federal, state, county, and municipal. Governmental bodies, unlike corporations, do not seek to make a profit; however, they need to make the most efficient use of tax dollars while providing all the services their citizens require. Employees with financial expertise are needed to do this. Small towns, like small corporations, may rely on only one employee—the treasurer or finance director—to manage all financial matters. Larger units of government, however, have financial operations that are just as complex, challenging, and highly staffed as those in large corporations.

Government treasury staffs are responsible for collecting tax revenues and for investing this money on a short-term basis, much as a corporate cash manager would. Governments also finance many of their projects and operations by issuing bonds that are paid back from future tax revenues and fee collections. Here, as in the corporate sector, public finance officers work with investment bankers to develop bond offerings. These offerings often are structured more creatively than those in the corporate world—partly out of necessity—to comply with certain bodies' restrictions on bond issues while conceiving securities that are attractive to investors and provide a good rate of return. "Some of the most innovative types of debt structuring are done in government," says Gary, a public finance veteran with decades of experience.

Gary's specialty, pension fund management, is also important to governmental bodies. The largest cities and states have pension funds as great as or greater than those of major corporations. Large cities such as Los Angeles and New York have billions in pension assets. Also, many government pension funds have grown faster than their corporate counterparts. The means of investment management, however, are much the same for government or corporate pension funds—investment in a variety of securities by either a group of in-house personnel or external investment management firms.

Another type of public finance job involves advising mayors, city managers, governors, county executives, or other top government officials on budget matters—basically, how much revenue is expected and how the government should spend it. There is also a variety of accounting, auditing, payroll, and risk management jobs to be performed for government bodies.

Entry-level government finance jobs tend to be administrative in nature, and the degree of specialization increases at higher levels. Those interested in public finance should get into the field early in their careers—governments tend to promote from within.

Employee Qualifications and Characteristics

A bachelor's degree is sufficient for most entry-level government finance jobs; candidates with degrees in business or public administration have a slight edge over liberal arts majors. An MBA may enhance an applicant's employability in a tight job market. Experience counts; the Government Finance Officers Association (GFOA) suggests that those who want to obtain advanced degrees pursue them while working in an entry-level job.

The GFOA urges undergraduates to seek public finance experience through internships or volunteer work.

Important characteristics for public finance professionals include communications and analytical skills, computer literacy, a sense of loyalty, and the ability to be a team player.

Salaries

Public sector salaries vary widely. Table 2.3 gives average salaries for chief financial officers in municipal and county governments.

Entry-level salaries often are competitive with those offered by corporate employers but they do not rise as high when an employee moves up the career ladder. The public sector offers excellent fringe benefits, however, and layoffs are rare. There is also the opportunity to deal with social issues that affect many lives. "You have a chance to work on things that you go home and see on the news," says Gary.

Finance in Academia

Institutions that specialize in the pursuit of knowledge are not exempt from the pursuit of dollars and cents. Colleges and universities have substantial endowment funds to be invested. They need lines of credit and other services from commercial banks to help fund various operations.

Table 2.3 Average Salaries for Municipal and County Public Officials (Chief Financial Officers) Region

Region	Mean Salary
New England	$66,833
Mid-Atlantic	$65,755
East North-Central	$65,929
West North-Central	$62,223
South Atlantic	$66,616
East South-Central	$62,796
West South-Central	$62,320
Mountain	$70,702
Pacific Coast	$89,211

Source: International City/County Management Association, Compensation 2003

Public colleges and universities may issue bonds to finance special projects, and all institutions must deal with budget and payroll activities.

The top finance employee at a college or university usually has the title of vice president for finance, or treasurer. This person may also be the chief investment officer, but in larger institutions, that may be a separate function. Depending on the size of the institution, there may be various assistant vice presidents, assistant treasurers, investment managers, analysts, and administrative personnel.

Investment of the endowment fund is a major function at most schools. An endowment is designed to provide a perpetual source of income for the institution; ideally, there is no need to dip into the principal (the original capital) of the fund. The investment income is exempt from taxes. The chief investment officer and his or her staff invest the endowment in much the same way as a corporate or public pension fund would be handled. The money may be allocated among a variety of instruments—stocks, bonds, real estate, venture capital—and is invested by either in-house personnel or a group of outside portfolio management firms that are monitored by the staff. Naturally, the institution will have a larger staff if it keeps the investment activity in-house. Some schools find hiring in-house investment personnel cost-effective because of the savings on fees to outside firms and because in-house managers often produce superior investment results. Good investment performance by the endowment can help schools in a variety of ways, such as by staving off tuition increases.

Investment staffs at some schools may be responsible for employee pension funds as well. Many colleges and universities, however, have their employee pensions handled through the Teachers Insurance and Annuity Association–College Retirement Equities Fund (TIAA–CREF), a large investment organization based in New York.

College and university finance personnel also deal with commercial banks to obtain lines of credit, set up accounts, and arrange any other services that are needed. There may be occasional needs to buy or sell real estate on behalf of the institution. Public institutions may issue bonds to fund expansion or special programs; finance personnel work with investment bankers to set bond maturities, interest rates, and other details of the offerings.

Other financial assignments within colleges and universities include drafting budgets (usually subject to the approval of the school's board of trustees or, in public institutions, a governmental body). Overseeing the issuance of payroll checks and bill payments and supervising the collection of tuition, fees, and other payments owed to the school are also functions of college and university finance personnel.

Employee Qualifications and Characteristics

Finance professionals in higher education tend to have MBA degrees and some experience with another employer, such as a bank or insurance company. Some also hold doctorates, although this is not normally a requirement. Personal qualities needed for the field include curiosity, tenacity, integrity, a sense of humor, and a willingness to work hard. Another key trait is the ability to take the long-term view of investment and other financial decisions and not worry about short-term market blips. Being able to take such a view also is one of the advantages of working in academia.

Salaries

Salaries usually are below those in the corporate sector; however, a job in higher education offers other advantages. Vacations and health benefits are usually good, there is easy access to high-quality cultural events and athletics, and there is exposure to the wide variety of people who populate academic institutions. According to the College and University Professional Association for Human Resources Administrative Compensation Survey, 2002–03, median salaries for chief financial officers in academia were $105,000 (large private institutions), $95,196 (large public institutions), $82,280 (private religious institutions), and $78,300 (two-year colleges).

Foundations

Foundations are charitable funds that are set up by individuals, families, or corporations to provide a source of donations to various causes. Foundations have been established with portions of some of the United States' greatest industrial fortunes, including the Rockefellers, Fords, and Mellons. Most foundations spread their grants among a variety of recipients—arts organizations, educational institutions, and the needy. A few are affiliated with a hospital or some other institution, and make all of their grants to it.

Investing is an important activity for foundations. Foundations are exempt from federal income taxes, but to maintain this status, they must give away 5 percent of their assets annually. Producing a return on investment that exceeds 5 percent is key to keeping the foundation's principal growing so that it will be available to generate investment income in the years ahead.

The chief financial officer or chief investment officer heads the investment operations and oversees a staff of investment managers and analysts. A large staff is needed if the foundation does its investing in-house; a smaller staff is sufficient if its main duty is to monitor outside portfolio management firms.

A foundation is also likely to employ staff accountants to maintain the books on investment activities, personnel to produce financial reports, and workers to handle noninvestment activities, such as payroll.

Employee Qualifications and Characteristics

Foundations, especially large ones, prefer to hire people with MBAs or other advanced degrees and who have some experience with other financial institutions. Some foundations have raised their salaries in recent years to compete with the rest of the financial world in attracting the most talented candidates.

Like endowments, foundations seek to hire people who are comfortable with a long-term investment orientation. They also look for individuals who work well as part of a team, are willing to work overtime when necessary, and are supportive of the foundation's mission. The idea of investing for a good cause is a factor that can serve to attract people to foundation work.

Salaries

In general, nonprofit salaries continue to be lower than those in the for-profit or government sectors. According to a survey by the *Nonprofit Times*, mean salaries for chief financial officers in nonprofit organizations in 2003 were $60,675. Overall, health benefits compare favorably with the other sectors, except for retiree coverage, which is generally less attractive in the nonprofit sector.

Keeping Hospital Finances Healthy

Hospitals must meet a variety of patient needs and, because of this, the institutions themselves have special financial requirements. Making money is not a concern for most U.S. hospitals, since the majority are run on a not-for-profit basis. Still, they face the challenge of financing the facilities, technology, and staff needed to provide high-quality patient care.

As in corporations, most hospitals have a chief financial officer who oversees all financial operations, ensuring that the hospital sticks to its mission and stays within budget. The CFO reports to the hospital's chief executive officer and board of directors and communicates frequently with the institution's chief operating officer and often the head of the medical staff.

A key officer working under the CFO deals with reimbursement for medical services, private insurance plans, Medicare, and Medicaid. This is complex and highly specialized work. The reimbursement officer identifies potential changes in reimbursements that result from new government regulations or other factors, such as contracts with insurers. Other responsibilities include reporting to Medicare officials and preparing information that is shared with the budget officer on the percentage of revenues that come from private and public insurance plans.

The budget officer fills another important role. This person generally prepares not only the budget for the current year, but also a five-year plan. The budgeting process involves input from heads of all departments within the hospital.

Hospitals sometimes have a controller to oversee the reimbursement and budgeting processes or other financial functions. Employees performing these other functions would likely be a general accountant, who takes care of payroll, accounts payable to vendors, and investment of short-term cash, and a patient accounting manager, who oversees the process of billing patients for services and obtaining payments from patients. The patient accounting manager also maintains information on what is owed to the hospital—and how this amount changes over time—and identifies overdue bills and other problem areas.

Some long-term financing and investing functions demand a team effort. Hospitals often issue bonds to finance new facilities or other improvements. Putting together the bond offerings usually involves the board of directors, CFO, controller, and budget and reimbursement officers. The controller and

CFO usually oversee the investment of employee pension funds or foundation money. Many hospitals have a foundation fund, which is used to finance various operations with its investment income.

General accounting is usually the easiest function for entry-level employees to handle. There is a possibility of entry-level employment in the budget area although it does require some knowledge of hospital operations. It generally takes four to five years to rise from an entry-level job to a supervisory position.

Employee Qualifications and Characteristics

A bachelor's degree in accounting, finance, or business management is good preparation for a hospital finance job. A master's degree is helpful for those who wish to rise through the ranks, and a certified public accountant designation is preferred for CFOs.

Some hospitals tend to promote from within; however, others may prefer outside experience—either with another hospital or in a corporation. A hospital financial career requires a somewhat different set of skills than a corporate one but most people can easily learn these skills.

A hospital environment requires a lot of flexibility. A manufacturer, for example, can precisely plan its output of product, but a hospital cannot always predict the number and type of patients it will admit or the treatment they will require. It is rare that two people will come to a hospital and receive the same services. Dealing with this unpredictability calls for adaptability on the part of the finance staff.

Salaries

Salaries for some hospital jobs may be less than for comparable corporate positions, although compensation for others may be a little more. For example, a hospital controller may make a somewhat lower salary than a corporate one, but salaries for reimbursement personnel may be attractive because the work is so specialized.

The Job Outlook

Hospitals provide a good career path as an alternative to corporate employment. Growth in the number of hospital financial positions available may be limited, however, because of the increasing use of automation for many functions.

CHAPTER

3

PORTFOLIO MANAGEMENT

Portfolio managers invest money in stocks, bonds, real estate, venture capital, and a variety of other instruments on behalf of their clients; many management firms specialize in one of these categories. Portfolio management firms may be part of a bank, an insurance company, or another type of company; or they may be independently owned. Some serve only large institutional clients, such as corporate and public pension funds, foundations, and endowments; others cater to a mix of institutions and individuals. Some serve individuals exclusively. Portfolio management firms offer lucrative career opportunities for a variety of people.

CAREER OPTIONS

Most portfolio management firms, or portfolio management departments within larger companies, have a wide range of jobs to fill. In a large firm or department, job responsibilities are highly specialized; in smaller operations, one person may undertake multiple assignments.

Portfolio Manager

At the heart of any portfolio management firm are the portfolio managers themselves—the people who actually make the decisions on the investments the firm will make. In large companies, these people may be vice presidents;

in small entrepreneurial operations, the president or chairman of the firm may be the sole, or at least the senior, portfolio manager. In many firms, the top portfolio manager is called the chief investment officer.

Most portfolio managers must make their investment decisions within the framework of the firm's overall investment policy; examples might be buying stocks in companies that are likely to grow rapidly in the next few years, or buying high-grade commercial real estate.

Employee Qualifications and Characteristics

Persons hired as portfolio managers usually hold an advanced degree in a related area, such as a master's degree in economics or an MBA with a concentration in finance. Firms that are "quantitative"—that is, rely heavily on computers to assist with investment decisions—often hire people with an engineering background or a master's degree in both engineering and finance.

Research Analyst

Portfolio managers generally rely on a team of research analysts for information to guide their investment decisions. Analysts look at factors that may make an investment good or bad. These factors include the financial condition of a company whose stock the firm may buy, the outlook for a company's product sales, and the company's competition, management, and labor relations. Analysts in quantitative firms may focus on a series of mathematical equations that determine if a security's value is likely to increase, or on factors that affect the stock or bond market as a whole. Some portfolio management firms do not employ analysts at all. Instead, they buy analysts' information from brokerage firms that have research departments or from investment-rating firms that specialize in this area.

Employee Qualifications and Characteristics

Research analysts, like portfolio managers, often have MBA degrees. Many firms encourage their analysts to complete the training necessary for a *certified financial analyst* designation as well. Quantitative firms may prefer analysts with Ph.D.s in fields such as economics or finance; often these employees are former college professors.

Trader

Trading is a significant function at portfolio management firms that invest in publicly traded securities, including stocks and bonds. For venture capital and real estate investments, arrangements to buy or sell are usually negotiated privately between the interested parties. Traders at portfolio management companies communicate with brokerage firms to arrange the purchase or sale of securities, as mandated by the portfolio managers' decisions. Also, in the 1980s and 1990s, a few large portfolio management firms began conducting a portion of their trades directly with other large investors, bypassing the brokerage community and securities exchanges. It is unlikely that the majority of trades will ever be done in this fashion—it's not always possible to buy or sell the stock you want without going to the floor of a stock exchange. The trades that are being carried out in this manner are one example of how trading is becoming an increasingly complex and challenging job. In addition, portfolio management firms are more aware than ever that investment results depend not only on selecting the right securities but also on buying or selling them at the most favorable time and price—down to fractions of seconds and fractions of dollars.

Employee Qualifications and Characteristics

Portfolio management firms are requiring more and more education and skills of the people who staff their trading desks. Although it was once common to find people without a formal education in these jobs, it is now typical for these positions to go to candidates with master's degrees, especially in large firms. An MBA or a master's degree in physics, computer science, or mathematics is good preparation for a trading-desk position. Extensive knowledge of computer technology is generally a plus for traders, especially in quantitative firms.

Marketer

As with all aspects of financial services, marketing plays a crucial role at portfolio management firms. In addition to actually selling the firm's services, marketers are responsible for communicating with existing clients and determining the firm's overall marketing strategy. This includes selecting the type of potential client the firm will target and the means it will use to present its services.

Employee Qualifications and Characteristics

Marketing staffs come from a wide variety of backgrounds. Although many firms hire people with MBAs in senior marketing positions, marketing staffs may also include people with liberal arts degrees. The most important trait of a good marketer is the ability to communicate—to understand complex investment concepts and explain them in simple terms.

Attorney

Most large investment firms have a department that deals with legal issues and compliance with regulatory agencies such as the Securities and Exchange Commission (SEC). This department often includes at least one lawyer and several professional staff members with training in public policy or a related area. Small firms generally hire outside legal help.

Operations Manager

Rounding out the employees in portfolio management is the operations manager, who handles all of the day-to-day aspects of running a business. Responsibilities include finding and renting suitable office space, purchasing computers and other office equipment, billing clients, and paying employees. The area of operations is becoming increasingly important as companies seek to improve their efficiency.

Employee Qualifications and Characteristics

Lower-level operations jobs are available to people without extensive education (perhaps just a high school diploma). For higher-level positions, candidates with college degrees or other training in business management generally are preferred.

The Job Outlook on Portfolio Management Careers

The outlook for employment opportunities in portfolio management is mixed. The number of jobs with firms that primarily serve institutional investors will grow slowly, if at all, and may even contract in the next few years. The market these firms serve is large and mature, but not growing substantially. Also, firms are making greater use of technology in an effort to find less labor-intensive ways to invest, and clients' substantial assets and financial clout are pressuring the firms to keep their fees down. Still, institutional investment management is a solid business. The market is clearly defined and the need for the service will always be there.

Because of the tough job market today, some people may have to start out in lower-level positions than when the industry was growing more rapidly.

An area of portfolio management that is expanding is the mutual fund industry. Some institutions invest through mutual funds; however, the funds' primary market is individuals. Mutual funds pool investors' money, allowing for greater efficiency in investing. Fund values are quoted daily on the financial pages of major newspapers. Many individuals who have been unsatisfied when investing through other vehicles are turning to mutual funds because of the funds' professional management. These customers also like the ease with which they can follow the funds' performance: through the Internet, newspaper reports, or the funds' customer service representatives.

Investors' satisfaction with mutual funds have also made them a popular vehicle for certain types of institutions (for example, pension funds in which the employee, not the employer, makes the investment choices). Employees tend to be familiar and comfortable with mutual funds and are happy to direct their retirement dollars there.

According to the Investment Company Institute's official survey of the mutual fund industry, the combined assets of the nation's mutual funds had reached $7.235 trillion in November 2003. This included stock funds, hybrid funds, taxable bond funds, municipal bond funds, taxable money market funds, and tax-free money market funds.

THE GLOBAL PERSPECTIVE

In typical investment industry parlance, an international firm invests outside its home country and a global firm invests both domestically and internationally. Both types of firms are growing, as new financial markets spring up around the world and improved information technology makes cross-border investing easier than ever.

There are some special qualities required for success in this business. "The most important criterion is complete flexibility," says Gavin, president of a successful global investment firm. The variables one encounters in international/global investing are almost infinite in number, he states. Every bit of international news can affect markets, and the people investing the money must make inferences about just what the effect will be. "Nothing is irrelevant," Gavin says. "You've got to be an inferential thinker. That's a skill you learn over time."

The need for intellectual flexibility also comes into play, according to Gavin, because it is important for people in any position to understand the functions performed by others in their firm. Those who do the investing should know what it is like to market the service; those in marketing should have a clear understanding of the investment process. This is desirable in any portfolio management firm, but crucial in the complex world of international and global investing. Fostering good communication and understanding within the firm will help it maintain good communication with clients. This is important because as the investment process becomes increasingly complex, clients demand more information.

Employee Qualifications and Characteristics

A bachelor's degree followed by an MBA degree, and ideally a chartered financial analyst (CFA) designation, can provide good preparation for work with an international or global firm. Knowledge of world cultures and currencies and daily attention to international political and economic news will also prove helpful. In some cases, foreign language skills may be needed. For all positions except those at the entry level, some previous related experience will be expected, even if not for a firm with an international focus.

Salaries

Salaries in international or global firms vary widely. In most cases, they tend to be results oriented. A person with an MBA degree may be hired for $30,000, $40,000, or $50,000 and not see substantial increases unless his or her performance is outstanding. Stellar performers, however, could see their salaries quintuple within five years.

INVESTMENT CONSULTING

Investment consulting is not the same as portfolio management but it is a related aspect of the business. Consultants help clients—mostly institutional investors—select, monitor, and evaluate the portfolio management firms they use. Consultants also help clients plan their larger investment strategies, such as what percentage of assets should go to stocks, bonds, real estate, or other classes of investments, and what approaches to investing should be employed within those classes. Some consulting firms have begun doing extensive research on what makes financial markets work the way they do.

Investment consulting as a formal defined business has been around only since the 1970s. It has grown because of the increased sophistication of institutional investors and because of the enactment of laws such as the Employee Retirement Income Security Act (ERISA), which set standards for the investment of pension funds. Not all institutions use consultants but a large number of them either keep a consulting firm on retainer or call on consultants for individual projects, such as the selection of a certain type of portfolio management firm.

People desiring a consulting career are advised to enter the field right out of college. This is because consulting firms tend to promote from within the company or business. Consultants must look at investing more in terms of the long-run big picture than do portfolio managers, who are oriented toward the day-to-day details of investing.

Entry-level professional jobs in consulting firms generally entail gathering and analyzing data on types of investments and investment firms and the production of reports on those topics. Two career paths may be taken from there. One path is to the highly visible position of account executive who interacts with the firm's clients, delivering to them any and all necessary services. Account executives usually have marketing responsibilities and seek out new clients for the firm. The other path leads to what some people call "scientific" positions. People in these jobs do complex and far-reaching research on such topics as what makes the markets tick and what mix of investments is most likely to produce the best results for a given investor. On both of these paths, people can rise to the level of senior consultant or officer of the firm. Each of these positions includes supervisory duties and a high degree of responsibility for the success of the enterprise.

Account executives should be good at sales and client service and possess a general understanding of the scientific aspects of the business. They also need to be skillful at negotiating contracts with clients. The "scientists" should have extensive analytical skills and enjoy the intellectual and theoretical elements of consulting.

Employee Qualifications and Characteristics

An MBA degree is good preparation for work in consulting; however, there is no need to feel overqualified. In a successful firm, it is possible to stretch a job's responsibilities to suit the employee's skills. Consulting firms are also expanding the services they offer to keep up with the growing complexity of investing; the more services a firm offers, the more valuable it is to its clients.

Also important are good oral and written communication skills. Since consultants are seen as "experts" by others, they must speak and write in an authoritative manner.

Salaries

Salaries in the consulting business vary widely. Beginning salaries of anywhere from $35,000 to $60,000 are typical, rising to six figures for a firm's senior-level employees.

The Job Outlook

Because of the expansion of services in many consulting firms, jobs in consulting will continue to be available for those with the necessary credentials. Some small firms may fail, but the larger players that dominate the business will grow.

FINANCIAL PLANNING

Another career related to portfolio management is personal financial planning. Planners offer a broad range of services aimed at helping individuals manage their financial lives.

Planners usually look first at an individual's program for retirement—at what age the person wants to retire, the level of income desired, and the amount of that income that will come from employer pensions or Social Security, savings, or investments. The planner also examines the client's other objectives; for example, to finance a child's college education, to travel extensively, or to take a sabbatical from work. The planner also determines if the client is properly insured or needs to make a new will. From here, the planner recommends a savings and investment strategy designed to meet the client's goals. Investments that a planner might recommend might include mutual funds, bank certificates of deposit, annuities purchased from insurance companies, or individually managed portfolios of stocks and bonds.

Some personal financial planners work for brokerage firms; however, the majority are self-employed, often working from a one-person office or perhaps with a small support staff. They come from a variety of backgrounds—some may be former accountants, securities analysts, stockbrokers, or corporate executives. In addition to having an understanding of finance, planners must be able to market themselves and to handle the day-to-day administration of a small business.

"You have to like working with people on a one-to-one basis," says Ron, a New York financial planner. "You have to like financial calculations; be comfortable working with numbers, tax laws, insurance; and enjoy helping people." Ron notes that he went into the field after being dissatisfied with a program another planner had designed for him. Before starting his planning practice, he worked in engineering and finance positions for a major corporation.

Financial planners who give investment advice, as many do, are required to register as investment advisers with the Securities and Exchange Commission. Some planners select the chartered financial consultant designation, which is insurance oriented. A course of study for that designation is available from American College, an insurance school in Bryn Mawr, Pennsylvania.

Membership in a professional association is a good way for planners to keep up on developments in their field. These organizations include the Institute of Certified Financial Planners, National Association of Personal Financial Advisors, and International Association for Financial Planning.

In the past few decades, some colleges and universities have begun to offer degree programs in financial planning and a related area, financial counseling. Purdue University in Lafayette, Indiana, was among the first; it began offering a bachelor's degree in financial counseling and planning in 1978.

Salaries

According to the Association of Financial Planners, professionals in this field can achieve excellent incomes. This income can be earned in a number of different ways, and as a result salary averages may not be as meaningful as for many other career areas. Experienced planners may earn well over $100,000 annually.

Planners may collect fees charged to their clients based on an hourly rate, a flat rate per plan, a percentage of the value of the client's assets or income, or a combination of such methods. They may also receive commissions from investment or insurance companies for products sold as a plan is implemented, or earn a combination of fees and commissions. Some financial planners are paid salaries by financial organizations or other institutions.

The Job Outlook

The employment of financial planners is expected to grow rapidly in the future, for a number of reasons. More funds should be available for investment as the economy, personal income, and inherited wealth grow.

People with financial planning training are likely to find many varied career opportunities. Some will advise affluent individuals, but others may focus on financial counseling—helping people from all socioeconomic groups with major financial decisions or crises. The U.S. armed forces make financial counselors available on military bases for servicepeople and their families who may need assistance. Financial counselors may work in hospitals, helping patients file insurance claims and work out payment plans for noncovered expenses. Directing finances for corporations or nonprofit organizations is yet another career path for persons with training in financial planning and/or counseling.

As awareness of the applications for this training grows, so will the opportunities for financial planning graduates.

C H A P T E R

4

INVESTMENT BANKING

One of the most demanding, lucrative, and glamorous aspects of financial services is investment banking. These firms help their clients—both corporations and governmental units—raise capital through the issuance of stocks and bonds. The firms underwrite the securities, help to promote them to potential investors, develop new types of securities and advise clients on their uses, and counsel clients on mergers, acquisitions, and other actions that are likely to have an impact on finances. The business contracted somewhat after its heyday in the middle 1980s and gave way to falling stock prices and recession. In the 1990s, however, it made somewhat of a rebound. The field of investment banking continues to attract graduates of top business schools in the United States.

Full-service investment banks also have brokerage divisions that trade stocks, bonds, commodities, and other financial instruments, both for clients and the bank's own account. (We will discuss this activity in Chapter 5.) This chapter will focus on underwriting and its related activities, including mergers and acquisitions.

UNDERWRITING

An investment bank underwrites a securities issue when it buys the entire issue from its client and resells the securities to the investing public. Underwriting is a huge business. The total amount of public equity (stock) and debt (bonds) underwritten in the United States for corporations totals in the trillions of dollars. Underwritings of private placements (equity and debt not sold to the general public but offered to a limited group of investors) and municipal bonds (issued by state and local governments) total several hundred billion dollars.

MERGERS AND ACQUISITIONS

Mergers and acquisitions make up a significant business for investment banking firms, although the activity has slowed somewhat. Leveraged buyouts (LBOs, or corporate takeovers that are financed by borrowing) were especially popular at one time. LBOs fell out of favor, however, because of large debts companies found themselves saddled with and because of problems in the market with "junk bonds" (debt securities that carry high interest payments and that are issued by companies deemed to be big risks by the investment community). There is still a demand for advisers to companies interested in buying others, but most companies are cautious about these actions and less willing to go into debt to finance them.

On the Job

People who work in the investment banking industry often start as financial analysts. These analysts research clients for which the bank is underwriting issues, consider various financing alternatives, and help develop clients' strategies. Most major Wall Street firms will hire a recent college graduate as an analyst, who may work for two or three years before going to graduate school for an MBA. After completing the MBA studies, the analyst has the combination of education and experience needed to move into a higher position with the firm. (Many investment banks will help promising employees pay for graduate school.) After receiving the MBA, an analyst is usually promoted to the position of associate. With additional experience, she may rise to vice president or partner in the firm.

As investment banking professionals move up, they have an increased amount of contact with clients, more responsibility for developing and maintaining those relationships, and the authority to advise clients on the appropriate type of financing for their needs. Financing options include whether to issue stock, bonds, or a hybrid type of security such as convertible bonds, which can be converted to stock. When the choice is bonds, a question arises as to what interest rate the securities should pay. There are some recent innovations in this area; namely, a few corporations have issued bonds whose rate of return is tied to outside factors, such as commodity prices. Another innovative type of financing in the past few years is asset-backed securities—bonds whose repayment is tied to some asset of the issuer. One example of an asset is payments the company expects to receive from its credit-card holders. Many investment banking professionals work on creating these new types of securities and on publicizing all the firm's security issues to the investment community.

In the mergers and acquisitions area, investment bankers advise clients on whether the transaction would be a good business decision by asking the following questions: Do the merging companies' product lines complement one another? Does the company to be acquired have excessive debt, labor problems, or other difficulties that could mean trouble for the buyer? Can the buyer afford the purchase? The investment banking firm also counsels clients on the best way to finance an acquisition or merger and may underwrite securities to be used for this purpose.

Employee Qualifications and Characteristics

Investment banking firms look for strong analytical skills in potential employees. Excellent oral and written communications skills are required as well as a great deal of ambition. This ambition, however, should not be the desire to be an individual "star"; investment banking is—above all—a team effort that requires a lot of energy. Workweeks of eighty hours or more are not uncommon.

Salaries

Investment banking professionals are well compensated for their long hours. People joining firms in analyst programs—just after receiving their bachelor's degrees—are likely to make between $30,000 and $50,000 a year. MBAs can expect salaries of $60,000 to $100,000 or more, plus bonuses. Compensation in the six-figure range is not uncommon, even during the early years of one's career.

JOB OUTLOOK

Like other segments of financial services, investment banking is becoming a global business. Overseas, many companies that once were government owned are now switching over to investor ownership. As a result, numerous new companies are growing to substantial size, especially in developing nations. This all creates the need for investment banking services. Many opportunities are now available and will go to people with a global outlook on business and foreign language skills.

According to the Department of Labor, demand for financial analysts should remain strong in the investment banking field, where they will be needed to assist new high-technology companies in raising money. In addition, the number of mergers and acquisitions taking place in the economy is not expected to slow down appreciably, so financial analysts will be needed to assist with such activities. Potential applicants should realize that competition for entry-level analyst positions in investment banking typically is intense, as the number of applicants usually far exceeds the number of vacancies.

CHAPTER 5

TRADING

After a portfolio manager makes a decision to buy or sell a security, it is up to trading desk personnel at brokerage firms and on the trading floors of exchanges to execute that decision. Trading encompasses not only stocks and bonds, but a variety of related instruments as well, including options and futures, which allow an investor to bet on the future direction of the stock and bond markets. Trading also involves agricultural commodities, energy products, and precious metals. Advances in telecommunications and computer technology have had a huge impact on trading, making it possible to conduct transactions around the clock in international markets. High pressure by nature, the world of trading is challenging and rewarding for those suited to it.

THE BROKERAGE FIRM

Almost all securities trades involve a brokerage firm. Many investment banking firms have a brokerage division, and there are many other brokerage firms that are independent companies. At brokerage operations that are part of investment banking firms, there is a strict division between the trading and underwriting areas to prevent the brokerage side from using confidential information to make trades in securities of companies that are receiving underwriting services. Brokerage operations affiliated with major Wall Street investment banks are some of the largest in the business. There are similarities in job functions, however, no matter what the size of the firm.

On the Job

Trading personnel at brokerage firms take orders to buy or sell securities on behalf of a wide variety of clients: portfolio management firms, pension funds and other institutions with in-house portfolio management operations, individuals, and, in some cases, the brokerage firm itself. Trading on behalf of portfolio management firms, pension funds, and other large financial institutions is called institutional trading (or institutional brokerage). Transactions made for individual investors come under the heading of retail trading or brokerage. Trading for the firm's own account is called proprietary trading.

For all types of clients, the brokerage firm has one overriding responsibility: to conduct the trade at the most advantageous price. This means trading personnel must monitor market movements closely and be extremely cautious about entering a market at times when an order to buy might drive a security's price up, or when an order to sell will push it down.

Brokerage firms generally have junior, intermediate, and senior levels of responsibility for trading personnel. Junior traders may execute the most straightforward transactions; complicated trades are handled by the intermediate or senior personnel. At the intermediate level, brokers usually have the duty of cultivating client relationships. Senior-level personnel are charged with planning overall trading strategy. According to the Securities Industry Association, a junior position requires three years' experience or less; an intermediate one demands four to six years in the business; and a senior position calls for six years of experience or more.

For most trades of stocks, options, or futures, the personnel of a brokerage firm's trading desk phones in the order to one of the firm's floor brokers at a securities exchange. The floor broker has the final responsibility for executing the trade—finding someone who wants to buy what the broker's client is selling, or vice versa. At stock exchanges, the floor broker has to make all orders known to the specialist—a trader who is assigned to certain stocks and is responsible for keeping buy and sell orders in balance to assure an orderly market. A specialist may be employed by a brokerage firm or may trade for his own account. Other traders, called market markers, usually trade for their own accounts and supplement the specialist's role in balancing buy and sell orders.

Types of Trades

Some trades take place outside of securities exchanges. Some stocks are traded in the over-the-counter market. In this market, brokers are linked by computer, telephone, and other communications equipment through the National Association of Securities Dealers' NASDAQ system. Stocks traded over the counter tend to be those of newer or smaller companies than those listed on the New York Stock Exchange or other large exchanges. There are exceptions, however. Most brokerage firms are members of NASDAQ as well as the major stock exchanges. A membership gives a firm or an individual the right to trade on that exchange or system.

Bond trades do not take place on an exchange or even through a NASDAQ–type system. Bond traders usually do not match buyers and sellers directly because there is less of a continuous market for bond trading than for stocks. Usually, a brokerage firm will become the owner of the bonds for some length of time (a few hours to a few months); that is, buy the bonds from a client who wants to sell and hold them until another client wants to buy. In this type of trade, the brokerage firm is said to be acting as a principal in the transaction.

Trading positions require mathematical and analytical ability and a great deal of energy. The environment on a brokerage firm trading desk or an exchange floor is extremely fast paced, and good traders must remain calm under pressure. Those who are developing and maintaining relationships with clients need excellent communications skills.

Trading is a challenging activity that can be lucrative. The potential for high earnings means keen competition for securities sales positions, particularly in large firms. Table 5.1 details earnings by type of employer. Institutional investors have pressured brokerage firms to lower commis-

Table 5.1 Median Annual Earnings of Securities and Financial Services Sales Agents by Employer, 2000

Type of Employer	Earnings
Security and commodity services	$71,260
Security brokers and dealers	$69,550
Mortgage bankers and brokers	$39,740
Personal credit institutions	$37,690
Mortgage bankers and brokers	$36,590

Source: U.S. Department of Labor

sions, however, and some institutions have used crossing networks to conduct some of their trades directly with one another, bypassing the brokerage community entirely. At the same time, institutions are still willing to pay top dollar to have difficult trades executed, and an increased number of individual investors have come into the financial markets. These factors could offset the negative ones.

Brokerage firms employ people in many different positions to support and supplement trading activity. Research analysts—such as those who work at portfolio management firms—gather information on various companies, which often leads to a recommendation to buy or sell a certain security. Because of the research department's work, brokerage firms are able to offer clients investment advice as well as trading services. (Some brokerage firms, known as discount brokers, sell themselves on the basis that they do not provide advice and therefore charge a lower commission rate.) Other brokerage firms sell their research to portfolio management organizations.

The research function of brokerage firms is changing just as it is in portfolio management firms. There is increasingly less call for research on individual securities and more for complex analysis of why markets behave as they do and how they interact with one another. This means there will be a need for analysts whose training and skills are more quantitative than was common in the past. At the same time, these analysts must be able to effectively communicate their theories to the investing public.

Another crucial aspect of brokerage firms is operations and technology. Employees in this area keep track of security trades, maintain records of clients' accounts, post dividend and interest payments, and perform many other duties related to securities processing. Higher-level employees supervise those performing processing tasks, and some are involved in developing and maintaining sophisticated computer systems to improve the firm's trading efficiency.

Brokerage firms also require personnel to monitor the firm's compliance with regulations set by government agencies, such as the Securities and Exchange Commission and Commodity Futures Trading Commission, and self-regulatory bodies such as the National Association of Securities Dealers (NASD). Larger firms usually maintain an in-house legal staff as well.

The education required to work in a brokerage firm varies from one job to another. For trading personnel, many of the larger brokerage houses have active recruitment programs at graduate schools of business. Many people, however, have become successful traders without graduate degrees and, in some cases, without undergraduate degrees. This is particularly true of people involved in the futures and options markets. "If a person is intelligent and hardworking, there is nothing in this industry that can't be learned," says Seth, a futures portfolio manager who is also familiar with trading issues.

Many analysts have MBAs and some have Ph.D.s in finance. Most large investment banking firms have programs—similar to those for underwriting personnel—in which degreed analysts can gain a few years of experience in an entry-level position, then go back to school for an advanced degree and return to the firm in a higher position. Most analysts also have the chartered financial analyst (CFA) designation, obtained through a course of study and examinations administered by the Association for Investment Management and Research.

For entry-level operations posts, firms tend to hire people with bachelor's degrees in computer science, mathematics, or a variety of business disciplines. Master's or Ph.D. degrees in these areas are common for upper-level operations staff. A bachelor's or master's degree in political science or public policy is appropriate for compliance staff. Top legal staff members, of course, have law degrees.

Earnings

Median annual earnings of securities, commodities, and financial services sales agents were $56,080 in 2000, according to the U.S Department of Labor (see Exhibit 5.1). The middle half earned between $33,630 and $107,800. The lowest 10 percent earned less than $24,770; more than 10 percent earned $145,600 or more.

Stockbrokers, who provide personalized service and guidance with respect to a client's investments, are normally paid a commission based on the amount of stocks, bonds, mutual funds, insurance, and other products they sell. Commission earnings are likely to be high when there is a great deal of buying and selling, and low when there is a slump in market activity. Most firms provide sales agents with a steady income by paying a "draw against commission"—a minimum salary based on commissions they can be expected to earn. Securities and commodities sales agents who can provide their clients with the most complete financial services enjoy the greatest income stability.

Trainee brokers usually are paid a salary until they develop a client base. The salary gradually decreases in favor of commissions as the broker gains clients. A small but increasing number of full-service brokers are paid a percentage of the assets they oversee. This fee often covers a certain number of trades carried out for free.

Brokers who work for discount brokerage firms that promote the use of telephone and online trading services usually are paid a salary. Sometimes this salary is boosted by bonuses that reflect the profitability of the office. Financial services sales agents generally are paid a salary; however, bonuses or commissions from sales are starting to account for a growing share of their income.

SECURITIES EXCHANGES—ON THE FLOOR AND UPSTAIRS

Stocks, options, and futures exchanges are beehives of trading activity. The workers swarming in them include employees of brokerage firms (as discussed in the previous section), employees of the exchanges themselves (which this section will explore), and independent traders investing for themselves.

Floor personnel are highly visible exchange staff members. Anyone who has toured an exchange or has seen a trading floor on television has observed people trying to make order out of the apparent chaos of the trading process. Exchange employees who work on the trading floor keep track of the prices of securities and the trades that are made. They also keep traders informed of these developments and maintain records for the exchange. It is a hectic environment and one that requires a great deal of stamina, flexibility, a sense of humor, and mathematical ability.

The exchange offers a wealth of opportunities to just about anyone from any background. A job on the trading floor is an entry into the financial markets for many people with just a high school education. Exchanges hire some college graduates for these positions as well. Some exchanges have started to list certain jobs as "college preferred," in hopes of attracting employees who are open to continuing their educations.

Jobs "upstairs" from the trading floor are less visible but no less crucial to the exchanges. Employees in market surveillance and compliance monitor trading activity and investigate complaints of irregularities or abuses. They also ensure that member firms are generally following the rules of the exchange, self-regulatory bodies, and government regulators. These people come from a variety of backgrounds and, as is the case in brokerage and portfolio management firms, education in public policy and a general understanding of the financial markets is helpful.

Research departments at exchanges create new financial instruments. This area requires knowledge of what investors want and need, and the ability to come up with the best way to meet those needs. A master's degree or Ph.D. in economics is common for research personnel.

Marketing staffs promote the exchange and its various financial instruments to the investment and brokerage community. Some liberal arts graduates go into marketing but may find it helpful to have some training in finance; one has to understand a product in order to market it.

Like many other financial organizations, exchanges employ lawyers in their legal departments, computer experts in their systems departments, accountants in auditing, and a variety of nonfinancial personnel in such areas as human resources and public relations. Many exchanges also maintain continuing education departments, such as the Options Institute at the Chicago Board Options Exchange (CBOE). These departments are not common to other kinds of financial institutions. Continuing education departments provide educational seminars for member firms, the media, and other audiences and often offer classes taught by outside experts as well as staff instructors. Individuals with a background in employee development and training are prime candidates for staff positions.

People who want to work on securities exchanges are likely to find a growing job market in the next few years. Exchanges are continuing to come up with new financial instruments, especially in the options and futures areas; new instruments, in turn, bring new customers to the exchanges. Also, stock, options, and futures exchanges are growing rapidly outside the United States, and some of these foreign exchanges are forming alliances with U.S. markets, providing opportunities for people interested in the international aspects of the business.

SECURITIES SALES WORKER (STOCKBROKER)

When investors buy or sell stocks, bonds, or shares in mutual funds, they use the services of securities sales workers. These workers are also known as registered representatives, account executives, or customers' brokers.

Securities sales workers relay the customer's "buy" or "sell" orders to the floor of the appropriate securities exchange or to the firm's trading department and notify the customer of the completed transaction and final price. They also provide related services such as financial counseling, the latest stock and bond quotations, and information on financial positions of corporations whose securities are being traded.

Securities sales workers can help a client accumulate a financial portfolio of securities, life insurance, and other investments geared either to long-term goals such as capital growth or income or to short-term objectives. Some sales workers specialize in one type of customer, such as institutional investors, or in certain types of securities, such as mutual funds.

Beginners in this field spend much of their time searching for new customers. As they establish a clientele, they spend more time servicing their existing customers and less seeking new ones.

Securities sales workers are employed by brokerage firms, investment banks, and mutual fund firms. Most work for a few large firms that have offices in a number of cities.

Sales workers are usually employed in bustling, sometimes noisy offices. Beginners usually put in long hours until they acquire a clientele, and sales workers occasionally meet with clients on evenings or weekends. Many sales workers leave the field each year because they are unable to establish a large enough clientele.

Qualifications, Education, and Training

Selling skills and ambition are necessary for success as a securities worker. A sales worker should also be mature, well groomed, and able to motivate people. Many employers prefer to hire applicants who have had previous experience in sales or management positions.

Most firms prefer a college education. A liberal arts background in economics, prelaw, business administration, or finance is particularly helpful.

Most employers provide training to new sales workers to help them meet state licensing and registration requirements. In firms that are members of major exchanges, the training program lasts at least four months. In enterprises firms and mutual funds and insurance companies, training is shorter and less formal.

Almost all states require securities sales workers to be licensed. Licensing requirements usually include a written examination and the furnishing of a personal bond. Those who intend to sell insurance in addition to securities must be licensed for that as well.

Sales workers must be registered as representatives of the firm for which they work. To qualify, they must pass the General Securities Registered Representative Examination, administered by the National Association of Securities Dealers, Inc.

Potential and Advancement

Most experts predict that the number of securities and financial services sales agents will grow faster than the average for all occupations through

2010. Growth in the volume of trade in stocks over the Internet will reduce the need for brokers for many transactions, but the rapid overall increase in investment is expected to spur employment growth among these workers. A majority of securities and commodities transactions will still require the advice and services of qualified sales agents.

The increasing number and complexity of investment products, as well as the effects of globalization, should positively affect the demand for brokers. As the public and businesses become more sophisticated about investing, they are venturing into the options and futures markets. Brokers are needed to buy or sell these products, which are not traded online. Also, markets for investment are expanding with the increase in global trading of stocks and bonds.

Of course, the employment of brokers will be negatively affected if the stock market or the economy suddenly declines. Even in good times, turnover is relatively high for beginning brokers who are unable to establish a sizable clientele. Once established, securities and commodities sales agents have a very strong attachment to their occupation because of their high earnings and the considerable investment they have made in training. Competition usually is intense, especially in larger companies with more applicants than jobs. Opportunities for beginning brokers should be better in smaller firms.

ENTREPRENEUR ON THE EXCHANGE— THE INDIVIDUAL TRADER

To many observers, individuals who trade for their own accounts are the most glamorous and fascinating figures in the world of finance. Risking their own capital, sometimes making or losing millions of dollars in a single day, they are often seen as the last rugged individualists—the last true capitalists of the system.

Like many attractive professions, this one is a little less glamorous up close. Still, those who make a living trading for their own accounts say it is an exciting, fascinating, intellectually challenging career, as well as one that demands dedication, perseverance, and just plain hard work.

Bill is an example of someone who has made a successful career of trading for his own account. He majored in banking and finance and minored in economics in college, then worked for several years on the equity trading desks of a couple of brokerage firms before buying a membership, or "seat," of his own on the Chicago Board Options Exchange (CBOE). "Very early on in my career, I had the sense that I wanted to have my own business," he says. Bill saw great potential and momentum in the CBOE, which was in its infancy at the time. He believed buying a seat there was a better choice for him than, for instance, starting his own brokerage firm.

Today, he still trades what he started trading—options on McDonald's stock—and eight other stock options that are traded in the same "pit," or space on the exchange floor. (An option is a contract that gives the holder the right to buy or sell a security at a set price on or before a specified date; a future is a contract to buy or sell a security or commodity by a specified date at today's price.)

A typical working day for Bill starts at 6:15 A.M., when he picks up the records of his previous day's trading. He analyzes where he stands and comes up with a set of theories to guide his trading for that day, based on his view of the market and other economic factors. Trading begins at 8:30 A.M. and continues until 3:15 P.M. Bill usually spends the full trading day in the pit, sometimes with a break for lunch, sometimes not.

"The variety is enormous," he says of his work. "Every day, you're faced with a new set of decisions." Much of the pleasure in his work, he states, comes from matching wits with other traders. According to Bill, "It's very exciting and rewarding."

While there is great pressure in the business, he believes that one learns to operate in that environment or else gets out. A good trader must have the ability to stay focused despite all the noise and activity in the pit—"It's overwhelming for some people," says Bill.

Another trait needed for the work is mathematical ability. "If there's one thing people on the floor have in common, it's a facility for math," is Bill's opinion. Along those same lines, he comments that people who are good at games are likely to be good at trading because they are able to think tactically and strategically. The most important traits of all, he adds, are confidence and the ability to make decisions.

His college education and experience in working for brokerage firms helped him in his career, giving him an understanding of how financial markets work. There are other ways to obtain this knowledge, he points out. It can, for instance, be gained by several years of doing clerical work on the floor of an exchange. Also, MBA programs and undergraduate business courses touch on markets, and other avenues of study are springing up, notably the program at IIT's Stuart School.

Bill enjoys the entrepreneurial aspects of his work. He is able to see the fruits of his labors instantly, and knows he has to depend on no one but himself. "You're not a cog in a bigger wheel," he says. "The stakes are very, very high, but the psychic benefits are well worth it."

Some people, he realizes, are much more comfortable under a corporate umbrella—but he likes being where he is. "I love what I do," he states. "I genuinely am still excited about coming to work in the morning."

JOB OUTLOOK

According to the U.S. Department of Labor, employment in the securities and commodities industry is projected to rise at a more rapid rate than for the average of all industries through 2010. Such growth should be prompted by increasing levels of investment in securities and commodities in the global marketplace. As long as interest rates remain low and the stock market performs adequately, people will continue to seek higher rates of return by investing in stocks, mutual funds, and other instruments. Along with new job openings developing from this growth, a large number of opportunities will arise as people retire or leave the industry for other reasons.

Several trends also hold promise for growth in this area. As baby boomers reach their peak earning and saving years, many are investing in tax-favorable retirement plans, such as the 401(k) and the Roth IRA. These plans have been one of the major causes of huge inflows of money into the stock market and into mutual funds, and this trend toward saving for retirement is expected to continue.

In addition, although online trading will grow and reduce the need for direct contact with an actual broker, the number of securities sales agents is still expected to increase, as many people still are willing to pay for the advice that a full-service representative can offer. As the number of self-directed retirement plans expands and as the number and complexity of investments rises, individuals will require more help in managing their money.

The globalization of securities and commodities markets is also expected to fuel growth in this area, as the expansion of traditional exchange and trading boundaries into new markets in foreign countries continues.

CHAPTER

6

BANKS, SAVINGS AND LOANS, AND CREDIT UNIONS

Banking influences our daily lives. Almost everyone is familiar with the services that a bank, a savings and loan (S&L) association, or a credit union offers to consumers—checking and savings accounts; home, auto, and educational loans; and certificates of deposit. The highly sophisticated financing services that many of these institutions offer to corporate customers (especially large commercial banks) are not familiar to most people. Individuals who work in these institutions must combine an understanding of finance with excellent interpersonal skills.

THE COMMUNITY BANK AND BEYOND

Banks whose primary market is made up of consumers and small businesses are often called community banks. The community they serve may be a small town or a portion of a large city. Community banks and S&Ls provide many of the same services and have many of the same job functions. Originally, S&Ls were set up primarily to provide home mortgages, but they have expanded into other product lines.

Careers in Community Banking

Loan officers in community banks evaluate the creditworthiness of applicants seeking to buy or improve homes or small, "mom and pop" businesses, purchase cars or boats, finance college educations, or meet a variety of other needs. Depending on the size of the loan and the institution's policies, the loan officer may have authority to approve or deny the loan outright, or to make recommendations to the lending committee. Junior personnel working under the loan officers help process applications and perform routine credit checks. The top people in lending set policy to govern loan making and evaluate new loan markets for the institution to enter. In a related activity, credit and collection personnel oversee the collection of loan payments and make arrangements to deal with problem loans. In community banks and S&Ls, it is important for lending personnel to know the local region and its dominant businesses. In rural areas, a loan officer may concentrate on agricultural lending; in oil-rich locales, on energy loans.

Other professional positions in community banks and S&Ls include overseeing bookkeeping and accounting functions, supervising tellers' activities and other duties related to checking and savings accounts, managing credit card operations, and marketing institutions' products and services.

Employee Qualifications and Characteristics

Educational requirements vary widely from one institution to another. In small enterprises, a bachelor's degree is likely to be sufficient, and it might not even have to be in finance—some liberal arts majors have become successful loan officers.

Careers in Large Banks

Large banks have departments that offer the same services as community banks, but operate in many other lines of business as well. These banks serve big corporate customers who need not only the typical services—such as loans and checking accounts, but who also may utilize a variety of highly sophisticated and complicated products; for example, the purchase of receivables, such as the debt owed to a company by its credit card customers. The bank purchases the receivables at a discount, so the company is able to obtain cash immediately; the bank makes a profit by collecting the full amount of the receivables over time.

Private placement of corporate debt with investors is another service the bank may provide. Other services can be anything from the most mundane to the most sophisticated. Bankers who provide services to large corporate customers must understand each company's business and needs—as well as what differentiates one financial service from another—in order to recommend the appropriate services to the company.

Personal and corporate trust services form another major line of business for large banks. The bank holds the assets of individual trust funds, corporate pension funds, or educational endowment funds; keeps track of the investments made by the portfolio managers handling the fund; and reports to the customer on the activity in the account. Many trust departments provide portfolio management services, and some banks have gone beyond this by establishing separate subsidiaries for portfolio management.

Another activity of a major bank might include foreign exchange—the conversion of currency for corporate and individual customers. Major banks also handle corporate cash management (the collection and deposit of payments owed to companies) more quickly than a company could do for itself. Venture capital investing, corporate real estate lending, and loans to foreign businesses or governments are also services provided by major banks. Traveler's checks, cashier's checks, and other products are often supplied to smaller banks that are unable to offer them on their own.

Entry-level professionals in any area of banking are likely to do a great deal of statistical analysis of various transactions. This work aids senior employees, who have greater face-to-face contact with customers and the authority to advise them on the most appropriate financial services for their situation. Senior employee duties may also include product sales and product creation.

Employee Qualifications and Characteristics

Large banks may hire recent bachelor's degree recipients for analyst positions, promoting them after three or four years of experience to junior officer, then officer. An MBA degree may be crucial to promotion at some banks; however, a degree is not necessarily a guarantee of success. Recent college graduates need to learn the fundamentals of a complex business and can only "learn by doing."

Key traits for success in banking include critical thinking skills, common sense, attention to detail, the ability to juggle multiple tasks, intellectual curiosity, initiative, diligence, flexibility, the capacity to deal with ambiguity, a positive attitude, and excellent communications skills. Being able to get along with many people is crucial because a job in banking offers greater variety than many other professions. An executive with an industrial company deals only with that company's products and services, for example, but a banker does the same for many different companies.

Salaries

Bank salaries vary greatly from one institution to another. According to the U.S. Department of Labor, salaries for chief executive officers in commercial banks averaged over $120,000 in 2000. Many earned significantly more, especially those employed by large banks. Top officers at the biggest banks often receive six-figure salaries and may be eligible for bonuses. Banks generally are known for job security, an added attraction.

That security may have dwindled somewhat in recent years. As other financing options became available to their most creditworthy customers, banks started taking bigger risks and accepting lower profit margins to generate business. This resulted in financial difficulties for many banks, leading in some cases to mergers. Despite such situations, many job opportunities can still be pursued in the nation's banks.

A COOPERATIVE EFFORT: CREDIT UNIONS

Credit unions are also considered banks. They perform many of the same functions as banks and S&Ls, but differ because they are not-for-profit cooperatives and are owned by their depositors. They also offer many of the same career opportunities as banks and S&Ls, and although salaries—especially for top management—are lower, many credit union employees feel this discrepancy is offset by the satisfaction of working in an institution that emphasizes community service. From a practical standpoint, there are other reasons to pursue a career in credit unions: they comprise a fast-growing segment of the financial services industry and they tend to promote from within.

Credit unions are established to serve the employees of a certain company or to serve a larger community. They tend to emphasize consumer financial services—such as savings accounts; share drafts (which work like checking accounts); credit cards; and home, auto, and educational loans—rather than services to businesses. Everyone who saves money at a credit union is a shareholder in the institution; shareholders typically are referred to as members. Members have the right to vote on credit union policy and on the appointment of officers and may run for the board of directors. Table 6.1 details federal and state credit union activity in 2003.

The smallest credit unions—those with assets of less than $100,000—are often run from the treasurer's home. Larger credit unions, however, tend to have extensive staffs and highly trained, sophisticated management.

Credit union careers are often built on specialty areas. A career path in accounting, for example, starts with a basic bookkeeping position and leads an employee through progressively more complex accounting assignments to a supervisory position. In lending, an employee will start out processing loan applications and move up to loan officer or other management positions, approving or disapproving loans and establishing lending policy for the institution. In operations, an employee begins as a teller and later supervises other tellers or all aspects of customer service. Data processing is another facet of operations. An entry-level employee performs data entry while higher-level workers design, maintain, and evaluate computer systems.

Table 6.1 Facts About Federally Insured Credit Unions
As of June 30, 2003

Number of credit unions	9,529
Federal CUs	5,864
State CUs	3,665
Number of CU members (in millions)	81.8
Assets (in billions)	$599.2
Insured shares (in billions)	$521.2
Loans (in billions)	$353.8
Loan/share ratio (percent)	67.9

Marketing responsibilities vary widely from one credit union to another. At credit unions that serve just the employees of one company, the market is clearly defined and the institution may need little marketing expertise. Occasional direct-mail communications with members—such as reminders about members' meetings and so forth—may be all that's necessary. Credit unions that serve a larger community, however, need sophisticated marketers who can choose among the many means available to communicate with potential customers. Typically, people on marketing staffs in these credit unions design advertising and promotional campaigns, either entirely in-house or with the assistance of outside agencies. They also determine the best media outlets for those campaigns. Those in upper-level positions plan and oversee the institution's long-term marketing strategy.

Employee Qualifications and Characteristics

Recent college graduates can find entry-level credit union jobs in accounting, lending, operations, and marketing. For most of these jobs, a bachelor's degree (preferably in finance or a related discipline) is required. When considering employees for promotion into middle- or upper-management jobs, many credit unions prefer those with an advanced degree, such as an MBA. Individuals aspiring to these positions are wise to obtain an advanced degree while working at a credit union, so that their credentials reflect a combination of education and experience. Conversely, a bit of experience is helpful when seeking entry-level positions. Undergraduates can gain experience through summer jobs, internships, or volunteer work; many credit unions use volunteers.

People who work for credit unions must have the same understanding of finance they would need in a bank or other institution. Even though credit unions do not seek to make a profit, they must maintain prudent lending standards and efficient operations if they are to remain in business. Employees must, however, be comfortable with the public service emphasis of credit unions, an emphasis that has attracted people from other segments of financial services. Many people come into the credit union industry from banks, savings and loans, and other financial services companies.

Salaries

Industry growth, along with the community service focus, may lead some people to decide that credit unions are more appropriate for them to work in than some of the more lucrative segments of financial services. At the entry level, credit union salaries are likely to be competitive with those at other financial institutions. Upper-level salaries may not reach as high, however. For example, chief executive officers of banks and S&Ls may earn up to 50 percent more than their credit union counterparts.

Job Outlook

An attractive aspect of the credit union industry is its growth in recent years. Credit unions, which focus on consumer finance, are not likely to be exposed to such potentially destabilizing factors as overseas loans or large real estate deals. This means that they offer job security and, because they usually promote from within, good opportunity for advancement. The Credit Union National Association, based in Madison, Wisconsin, and state credit union leagues can provide additional information on employment with credit unions.

C H A P T E R

7

OTHER CAREERS IN FINANCE

Financial services professionals affect almost every aspect of business. From actuary to underwriter, this chapter explores many careers in the financial world that were not covered in detail in earlier chapters. Each career description includes detailed information, including job description; places of employment and working conditions; qualifications, education, and training; potential and advancement; and income.

ACTUARY

In general, actuaries are mathematicians. They assemble and analyze statistics on probabilities of death, illness, injury, disability, unemployment, retirement, and property losses to design insurance and pension plans and set up the premium structure for these policies.

For example, statistics on auto accidents are gathered and analyzed by actuaries employed by a company selling auto insurance. The actuaries then base the premiums for their company's policies on the accident statistics for different groups of policyholders. They consider age, miles driven annually, and geographic location, among other things.

Since the insurance company is assuming a risk, the premium rates developed by actuaries must enable the company to pay all claims and expenses and must be adequate to provide the company with a reasonable profit for assuming that risk. Actuaries must be up to date on general economic and social trends and on any legislative developments that might affect insurance practices.

Actuaries provide information to executives in their companies' investments, group underwriting, and pension planning departments; they prepare material for policyholders and government requirements; and they may be called on to testify before public agencies regarding proposed legislation on insurance practices.

Actuaries employed by the federal government usually work on a specific insurance or pension program such as Social Security. Those in state government positions regulate insurance companies, supervise state pension programs, and work in unemployment insurance and workers' compensation programs.

Consulting actuaries set up pension and welfare plans for private companies, unions, and government agencies. Some consulting actuaries evaluate pension plans and certify their solvency in compliance with the Employee Retirement Income Security Act (ERISA).

Private insurance companies employ over one-half of all actuaries, with life insurance companies employing the most. Large companies may employ over one hundred actuaries; many smaller companies use the services of consulting firms or rating bureaus. Other actuaries work for private organizations that administer independent pension or welfare plans, or for federal and state agencies.

Beginning actuaries often rotate among various jobs within a company's actuarial operation to become familiar with its different phases. In the process, they gain a broad knowledge of insurance and related fields.

Actuaries have desk jobs and usually work at least a forty-hour week. Occasional overtime is necessary.

Qualifications, Education, and Training

A strong background in mathematics is necessary for anyone interested in a career as an actuary.

Some colleges and universities offer degrees in actuarial science. A bachelor's degree with a major in mathematics, statistics, or business administration is also a good educational background for an actuary, however. Courses in insurance law, economics, and accounting are valuable.

Of equal importance as a strong mathematics background are the examination programs offered by professional actuarial societies to prospective actuaries. Examinations are given twice a year, and extensive home study is required to pass the more advanced ones. Completion of one or more of these examinations while still in school helps students evaluate their potential as actuaries; those who pass one or more examinations usually have better employment opportunities and receive higher starting salaries. Actuaries are encouraged to complete an entire series of examinations as early as possible in their careers to achieve full professional status. This usually takes from five to ten years.

Associate membership in their respective professional societies is awarded to actuaries after successful completion of half the examinations in the life insurance or pension series, or seven examinations in the casualty series. Full membership is awarded, along with the title "fellow," on completion of an entire series.

Consulting pension actuaries who service private pension plans and certify the plans' solvency must be enrolled and licensed by the Joint Board for the Enrollment of Actuaries, which stipulates the experience and education required.

Potential and Advancement

Actuaries held about 14,000 jobs in 2000, according to the Department of Labor. The majority who were wage and salary workers were employed in the insurance industry. Some had jobs in life and health insurance companies, while property and casualty insurance companies, pension funds, or insurance agents and brokers employed others. Most of the remaining actuaries worked for firms providing a variety of corporate services, especially management and public relations, or for actuarial consulting services. A relatively small number of actuaries were employed by securities and commodities brokers or by government agencies. Some developed computer software for actuarial calculations.

Advancement within the field depends on job performance, experience, and the number of actuarial examinations successfully completed. Actuaries can be promoted to assistant, associate, and chief actuary within their companies. Because they have a broad knowledge of insurance and its related fields, actuaries are often selected for administrative positions in other company departments such as underwriting, accounting, or data processing. Many actuaries advance to top executive positions, where they help determine company policy.

This occupation generates relatively few job openings from employment growth and the need to replace those who leave the occupation each year. Employment of actuaries is expected to grow more slowly than the average for all occupations through 2010, due to a slowdown in actuarial employment growth in insurance industries, which traditionally employ the majority of actuaries.

In the near future, new employment opportunities should become available in health services, in medical and health insurance industries, and in government—in health care and Social Security. Changes in managed health care and the desire to contain health care costs will continue to provide opportunities for actuaries. Some actuaries also are evaluating the risks associated with controversial medical issues, such as genetic testing or the impact of diseases such as AIDS. Others in this field are involved in drafting health care legislation. As health care issues and Social Security reform continue to receive growing attention, opportunities for actuaries should increase.

Actuaries will continue to be needed to evaluate risks associated with catastrophes, such as earthquakes, tornadoes, hurricanes, floods, and other natural disasters. Expanding areas in property and casualty insurance are environmental and international risk management. Actuaries evaluate risks such as the likelihood of a toxic waste spill, or the costs and benefits of implementing pollution control equipment in a factory. As economic globalization continues and companies expand their operations abroad, they increasingly rely on actuaries to evaluate the risk of setting up a new factory or acquiring a foreign subsidiary.

Additional jobs for actuaries should also be found in the banking and securities and commodities industries. As financial services continue to consolidate and insurance firms, banks, and securities firms enter one another's markets, new opportunities will emerge. Actuaries will be needed to analyze the risks associated with entering a new market, such as launching a new service or merging with an already established company. At the same time, changes in consumer preferences for retirement investment plans will adversely affect employment in the life insurance and pension funds industries. The overall decline in the life insurance industry, reflecting fewer life insurance policies sold in favor of investments earning higher returns, will continue to affect the need for actuaries. Similarly, more people are choosing to invest in defined contribution plans, which are less complicated to analyze and therefore require fewer actuaries than defined pension systems. Actuaries in the pension funds industry are more likely to be involved in financial planning—helping people manage their retirement money.

Income

According to the U.S. Department of Labor, median annual earnings of actuaries were $66,590 in 2000. The middle 50 percent earned between $47,260 and $93,140. The lowest 10 percent had earnings of less than $37,130, while the top 10 percent earned over $127,360.

The average salary for actuaries employed by the federal government was $78,120 in 2001. According to the National Association of Colleges and Employers, annual starting salaries for bachelor's degree graduates in actuarial science averaged $45,753 in 2001.

Insurance companies and consulting firms give merit increases to actuaries as they gain experience and pass examinations. Some companies also offer cash bonuses for each professional designation achieved.

UNDERWRITER

Because insurance companies assume millions of dollars in risks by transferring the chance of loss from their policyholders to themselves, they employ underwriters to study and select the risks the company will insure. Underwriters analyze insurance applications, medical reports, actuarial studies, and other material. They must use personal judgment in making decisions that could cause their companies to lose business to competitors (if they are too conservative) or to pay too many claims (if they are too liberal).

Most underwriters specialize in one of the three basic types of insurance: life, property and casualty, or health. Property and casualty underwriters also specialize by type of risk: fire, automobile, or workers' compensation, for example. Underwriters correspond with policyholders, insurance agents, and insurance office managers. They sometimes accompany salespeople as they call on customers and may attend meetings with union representatives or union members to explain the provisions of group policies.

Underwriters who specialize in commercial underwriting often evaluate a firm's entire operation before approving its application for insurance. The growing trend toward "package" underwriting of various types of risks under a single policy requires that the underwriter be familiar with several different lines of insurance rather than specialize in just one line.

Beginners work under close supervision of an experienced underwriters. They progress from evaluating routine applications to handling those that are more complex and have greater face value. Most underwriters are employed in the home offices of their companies, many of which are located in and around Boston, Chicago, Dallas, Hartford, New York City, Philadelphia, and San Francisco. Some are also employed in regional offices in other cities.

Underwriting is basically a desk job. The average workweek is thirty-five to forty hours, with occasional overtime required.

Qualifications, Education, and Training

A career as an underwriter can be very satisfying to someone who likes to work with details and who enjoys relating and evaluating information. Underwriters must be able to make decisions and communicate well. They must also be imaginative and aggressive when searching out information from outside sources.

Some small insurance companies will hire underwriter trainees without a college degree, although high school or postsecondary courses in mathematics are valuable. Large insurance companies require a college degree, preferably in finance or business administration.

As in all jobs in the insurance industry, great emphasis is placed on the completion of independent study programs throughout an employee's career. Salary increases and tuition costs are often provided by the company on completion of a course. Study programs are available through a number of insurance organizations and professional societies.

Potential and Advancement

Employment levels in this field are expected to remain stable through 2010. Most job openings are likely to arise from the need to replace underwriters who transfer or leave the occupation, although some new job openings are being created for underwriters in the area of product development. These underwriters help set the premiums for new insurance products, such as those in the rapidly growing field of long-term care insurance.

The best job prospects will be for underwriters with the right abilities and credentials, such as excellent computer and communication skills coupled with a background in finance.

Job prospects may be better in health insurance than in property and casualty and life insurance. As federal and state laws require health insurers to accept more applicants, the number of policies sold will increase. Also, as the population ages, there will be a greater need for health and long-term care insurance.

Since insurance is considered a necessity for people and businesses, there will always be a need for underwriters. It is a profession that is less subject to recession and layoffs than other fields. A broad knowledge of insurance is desirable, so that underwriters can transfer to another underwriting specialty if downsizing occurs.

Income

Labor department statistics reveal that median annual earnings of insurance underwriters were $43,150 in 2000. The middle 50 percent earned between $33,300 and $57,280 a year. The lowest 10 percent earned less than $27,280, while the highest 10 percent earned over $74,060. Median annual earnings in the industries employing the largest number of insurance underwriters in 2000 were:

Fire, marine, and casualty insurance	$44,360
Life insurance	$42,900
Insurance agents, brokers, and service	$42,140
Medical service and health insurance	$38,060

Insurance companies usually provide good benefits, including employer-financed group life, health, and retirement plans.

INSURANCE AGENT AND BROKER

Insurance agents and brokers sell insurance policies to individuals and businesses to protect against financial losses and to provide for future financial needs. They sell one or more of the three basic types of insurance: life, property-liability (casualty), and health.

An agent may be either the employee of an insurance company or an independent representative of one or more insurance companies. A broker is not under contract to a specific insurance company or companies but places policies directly with whichever company can best serve the needs of a client. Both agents and brokers spend the largest part of their time discussing insurance needs with prospective customers and designing insurance programs to meet each customer's individual requirements.

Life insurance agents and brokers (life underwriters) sell policies that provide payment to survivors (beneficiaries) when the policyholder dies. A life policy can also be designed to provide retirement income, educational funds for surviving children, or other benefits.

Casualty insurance agents and brokers sell policies that protect against financial losses from such mishaps as fire, theft, and automobile accidents. They also sell commercial and industrial insurance, such as workers' compensation, product liability, and medical malpractice.

Health insurance policies offer protection against the cost of hospital and medical care as well as loss of income due to illness or injury, and are sold by both life and casualty agents and brokers.

More and more agents and brokers are becoming multiline agents, offering both life and property-liability policies to their clients. Some agents and brokers also sell securities such as mutual funds and variable annuities, or combine a real estate business with insurance sales. Successful insurance agents or brokers are highly self-motivated. Anyone interested in this work as a career should be aware that many beginners leave the field because they are unable to establish a large enough clientele. For those who succeed, the financial rewards are usually very good. Related jobs are actuary, claim representative, and underwriter.

Places of Employment and Working Conditions

Insurance agents and brokers are employed throughout the country, in all locations and communities, but the largest number work in or near large population centers.

Agents and brokers are free to schedule their own hours but often work evenings and weekends for the convenience of their clients. In addition, hours devoted to paperwork and continuing education often increase the workweek to much more than forty hours.

Agents and brokers usually pay their own automobile and travel expenses. If they own and operate their own agencies, they also pay clerical salaries, office rental, and operating expenses out of their own incomes.

Qualifications, Education, and Training

Agents and brokers should be enthusiastic, self-confident, and able to communicate effectively. They need initiative and sales ability to build a clientele, and must be able to work without supervision.

Many insurance companies prefer a college degree (in almost any field) but will hire high school graduates with proven ability or outstanding potential. Courses in accounting, economics, finance, business law, and insurance are the most useful, whether the agent works for an insurance company or is self-employed.

New agents receive training at the agency where they will work or at the home office of the insurance company that employs them. All states require agents and brokers to be licensed. In most states, this entails completing specified courses and passing a written examination covering state insurance laws. Insurance companies often sponsor classes to prepare their fledgling agents for the licensing exam, while other new agents study on their own. Some trade and correspondence schools offer courses for insurance agents.

Agents and brokers who wish to succeed in this field are constantly studying to increase their skills; they take college courses and attend educational programs sponsored by their own companies or by insurance organizations. The Life Underwriter Training Council awards a diploma in life insurance marketing after successful completion of the council's two-year life program. The council also sponsors a program in health insurance. Experienced agents and brokers earn the chartered life underwriter (CLU) designation by passing a series of examinations given by the American College of Bryn Mawr, Pennsylvania. Property-liability agents receive the chartered property casualty underwriter (CPCU) designation in the same way from the American Institute for Property and Liability Underwriters.

Potential and Advancement

The federal government projects slower-than-average employment growth for insurance agents through 2010. Nevertheless, employment opportunities for agents will be favorable for persons with the right qualifications and skills.

Applicants who enjoy competitive sales work, have excellent interpersonal skills, and have developed expertise about a wide range of insurance and financial services will have the brightest prospects. Multilingual agents also should be in high demand because they can serve a greater number of customers. Most job openings are likely to result from the need to replace agents who leave the occupation and the large number of agent retirements expected in coming years.

In the future, demand for insurance sales agents will depend largely on the volume of sales of insurance and other financial products. Although sales of life insurance are down, rising incomes and a concern for financial security during retirement are lifting sales of annuities, mutual funds, and other financial products sold by insurance agents. Sales of health and long-term care insurance also are expected to rise sharply as the population ages and as the law provides more people access to health insurance. In addition, a growing population will increase the demand for insurance for automobiles, homes, and high-priced valuables and equipment. As new businesses emerge and existing firms expand coverage, sales of commercial insurance also should increase, including coverage such as product liability, workers' compensation, employee benefits, and pollution liability insurance.

Employment of agents is not expected to keep up with the rising level of insurance sales, however. As insurance companies attempt to reduce costs, many are relying less on agents working directly for insurance carriers and more on independent agents or direct marketing through the mail, by phone, or on the Internet.

Agents who incorporate new technology into their existing businesses will stay competitive, and those who are knowledgeable about their products and sell multiple lines of insurance and other financial products will remain in demand. Since most individuals and businesses consider insurance a necessity regardless of economic conditions, agents are not likely to face unemployment because of a recession.

Income

According to the Department of Labor, median annual earnings of wage and salary insurance sales agents were $38,750 in 2000. The middle 50 percent earned between $26,920 and $59,370. The lowest 10 percent had earnings of $20,070 or less, while the highest 10 percent earned more than $91,530. Median annual earnings in the industries employing the largest number of insurance sales agents in 2000 were:

Fire, marine, and casualty insurance	$46,320
Medical service and health insurance	$38,900
Insurance agents, brokers, and service	$38,470
Life insurance	$35,920

Many independent agents are paid by commission only. Sales workers who are employees of an agency or an insurance carrier may be paid a salary only, salary plus commission, or salary plus bonus. Commissions tend to be the most common form of compensation, especially for experienced agents.

The amount of commission depends on the type and amount of insurance sold, and whether the transaction is a new policy or a renewal. Bonuses are usually awarded when agents reach their sales goals or when an agency's profit goals are met. Some agents involved with financial planning receive a fee for their services rather than a commission.

Company-paid benefits to insurance sales agents may include continuing education, paid licensing training, group insurance plans, and office space and clerical support services. Some firms pay for automobile and transportation expenses, attendance at conventions and meetings, promotion and marketing expenses, and retirement plans. Independent agents working for insurance agencies receive fewer benefits, but their commissions may be higher to help them pay for marketing and other costs.

CLAIMS REPRESENTATIVE

Claims representatives, including both claims adjusters and claims examiners, investigate claims for insurance companies, negotiate settlements with policyholders, and authorize payment of claims.

Claims adjusters work for property-liability (casualty) insurance companies and usually specialize in specific types of claims such as fire, marine, or automobile.

They determine whether the company is liable (that is, whether the customer's claim is a valid one covered by the customer's policy) and recommend the amount of the settlement. In the course of investigating a claim, adjusters consider physical evidence, testimony of witnesses, and any applicable reports.

They strive to protect their companies from false or inflated claims and at the same time settle valid claims quickly and fairly. In some firms, adjusters submit their findings to claims examiners, who then review them and authorize payment.

In states with "no-fault" auto insurance, adjusters do not need to establish responsibility for a loss but must decide the amount of the loss. Many auto insurance companies employ special inside adjusters who settle smaller claims by mail or telephone or at special drive-in centers where claims can be settled immediately. Most claims adjusters are employed by insurance companies, but some work for independent firms that contract their services to insurance companies for a fee. These firms vary in size from local ones employing two or three adjusters to large national organizations with hundreds of adjustment specialists.

A few adjusters represent the insured rather than the insurance company. These "public" adjusters are retained by banks, financial organizations, and other businesses to negotiate settlements with insurance companies.

In life insurance companies, claims examiners are the equivalent of claims adjusters. In the course of settling a claim, an examiner might correspond with policyholders or their families, consult medical specialists, calculate benefit payments, and review claim applications for completeness. Questionable claims or those exceeding a specified amount are even more thoroughly investigated by the examiner.

Claims examiners also maintain records of settled claims and prepare reports for company data processing departments. More experienced examiners serve on company committees, survey claim settlement procedures, and work to improve the efficiency of claim handling departments.

Adjusters work in cities and towns of all sizes. Claims examiners, on the other hand, work at the home offices of insurance companies, many of which are located in and around Boston, Chicago, Dallas, New York City, Philadelphia, and San Francisco.

Typically, claims adjusters make their own schedules, doing whatever is necessary to dispose of a claim promptly and fairly. Since most firms provide twenty-four-hour claim service, adjusters are on call all the time and may work some weekends and evenings. They may be summoned to the site of an accident, fire, or burglary, or to the scene of a riot or hurricane. They must be physically fit since they spend much of their day traveling, climbing stairs, and actively investigating claims. Much of their time is spent outdoors—this is not a desk job.

Claims examiners, by contrast, do have desk jobs. Their usual workweek is thirty-five to forty hours, but they may work longer hours during peak claim loads or when quarterly and annual reports are prepared. They may travel occasionally in the course of their investigations and are sometimes called on to testify in court regarding contested claims.

Qualifications, Education, and Training

Claims representatives must be able to communicate tactfully and effectively. They need a good memory and should enjoy working with details. Claims examiners must also have mathematical skills and be familiar with medical and legal terms and insurance laws and regulations.

Insurance companies prefer to hire college graduates as claims representatives but will sometimes hire those with specialized experience, such as individuals with automobile repair experience for automobile claims adjuster positions.

Because of the complexity of insurance regulations and claim procedures, however, claims representatives without a college degree may advance more slowly than those with two years of college or more.

Many large insurance companies provide on-the-job training combined with home-study courses for newly hired claims adjusters and claims examiners. Throughout their careers, claims representatives continue to take a variety of courses and programs designed to certify them in many different areas of the profession.

Licensing of adjusters is required in most states. Requirements vary, but applicants usually must be twenty or twenty-one years of age and a resident of the state, complete an approved training course in insurance or loss adjusting, provide character references, pass a written examination, and file a surety bond (a bond guaranteeing performance of a contract or obligation).

Potential and Advancement

Claims adjusters, along with the related occupations of appraisers, examiners, and investigators, held about 207,000 jobs in 2000, according to the U.S. Department of Labor. Nearly 13,000 of these were auto damage insurance appraisers.

Almost all claims adjusters are employed by insurance companies. Other employers of these and workers in related positions include insurance sales agents and brokers and independent adjusting and claims processing firms.

Employment in this area is expected to grow about as fast as the average for all occupations through 2010. Opportunities will be best in the areas of property and casualty insurance and health insurance. Many job openings also will result from the need to replace workers who transfer to other occupations or leave the labor force.

Many insurance carriers are downsizing their claims staff in an effort to contain costs. Larger companies are relying more on customer service representatives in call centers to handle the recording of the necessary details of the claim, allowing adjusters to spend more of their time in investigation. New technology also is reducing the amount of time it takes for an adjuster to complete a claim, therefore increasing the number of claims one adjuster can handle. So long as insurance policies are being sold, however, there will be a need for adjusters, appraisers, examiners, and investigators. Despite recent gains in productivity resulting from technological advances, these jobs are not easily automated.

Income

Department of Labor figures reveal that earnings of claims adjusters, examiners, and investigators vary significantly. Median annual earnings were $41,080 in 2000. The middle 50 percent earned between $31,960 and $54,300. The lowest 10 percent earned less than $25,860, and the highest 10 percent earned more than $68,130. Earnings tended to be highest in fire, marine, and casualty insurance.

Claims adjusters and appraisers working for insurance companies tend to earn slightly higher average earnings than independent adjusters because they have a steady income. Many claims adjusters also receive additional bonuses or benefits as part of their jobs, as well as other benefits, such as a company car.

BANK OFFICER

Bank officers are responsible for carrying out the policies set by the board of directors of the bank and for overseeing the day-to-day operations of all the banking departments.

A thorough knowledge of both business and economics is necessary, plus expertise in the specialized banking area for which each officer is responsible.

Bank officers and their responsibilities include trust officer, who administers estates and trusts, manages property, invests funds for customers, and provides financial counseling; operations officer, who plans and coordinates procedures and systems; branch manager, who is responsible for all functions of a branch office; international officer, who handles financial dealings abroad or for foreign customers; cashier, who is responsible for all bank property; and loan officer (discussed in Chapter 6). Other officers handle auditing, personnel administration, public relations, and operations research. In small banks, there may be only a few officers, each of whom handles several functions or departments.

Bank officers are employed in towns and cities of all sizes throughout North America. More jobs are found in large cities, but many smaller communities also have banking institutions.

Normally, bank officers are involved in the civic and business affairs of their communities and are often called on to serve as directors of local companies and community organizations. This can entail evenings spent away from home attending meetings and functions related to these positions.

Qualifications, Education, and Training

The ability to inspire confidence in others is a necessary characteristic of a successful bank officer. Officers should also display tact and good judgment in dealing with customers and employees. The ability to work independently and to analyze information is also important.

High school students interested in banking should study mathematics and take any available courses in economics.

Potential bank officers usually start their careers by entering a bank's management training program after graduation from college. Occasionally, outstanding clerks and tellers work their way up the ladder through promotion and are also accepted into these training programs, but the usual background is a college degree. The ideal preparation for a banking officer has been described as a bachelor' degree in social science along with an MBA degree. A business administration degree with a major in finance or a liberal arts degree with courses in accounting, economics, commercial law, political science, and statistics are also good college background.

Potential and Advancement

Employment is expected to increase substantially in this field. Banking is one of the fastest-growing industries in our economy; expanding bank services and the increased use of computers will continue to require trained personnel in all areas of banking.

It usually takes many years of experience to advance to senior officer and management positions. Experience in several banking departments, as well as continuing education in management-sponsored courses, can aid and accelerate promotion.

Income

According to the U.S. Department of Labor, median annual earnings of financial managers in commercial banks were $55,960 in 2000.

Income levels for bank officers vary widely. Large banks and those located in metropolitan areas tend to pay higher salaries than those located in small towns, and earnings also vary, depending on the type of management position. For example, annual earnings for financial analysts in the banking industry were just over $47,500 in 2000, while for loan officers they were slightly more than $40,000.

BANK WORKER

Banks employ the same clerical workers as other businesses and industries—file clerks, word processors, administrative assistants, and receptionists. But there are two groups of employees that perform duties unique to the banking industry—clerks and tellers.

Bank clerks are responsible for all the records of the monetary activities of the bank and its customers. They have specialized duties and often use office machines that are designed especially for banking functions. Their titles include sorter, proof machine operator, bookkeeping machine operator, bookkeeping and accounting clerk, transit clerk, interest clerk, and mortgage clerk. With the wide use of electronic data processing equipment in the banking industry, bank clerk occupations also now include such jobs as electronic reader-sorter operator, check inscriber or encoder, control clerk, coding clerk, tape librarian, and teletype operator.

Tellers are the most visible employees of a bank and should project an efficient, pleasant, and dependable image, both for themselves and for their employers. Tellers cash checks, process deposits and withdrawals, sell savings bonds and traveler's checks, keep records, and handle paperwork. In the course of completing these tasks, they must be thorough and accurate in checking identification, verifying accounts and money amounts, and counting out cash to customers. At the end of their working day, all transactions must balance.

Some opportunities for part-time teller work exist in large banks. These extra tellers are used during peak banking hours and on peak banking days.

Bank clerks and tellers work in all areas of both Canada and the United States, in communities of all sizes. In smaller banks, clerks and tellers usually perform a variety of duties, while in larger banks they generally work in one specialty area.

Qualifications, Education, and Training

Personal qualities of honesty and integrity are necessary for a job in banking. A fondness for working with numbers, attention to detail, and the ability to work as part of a closely supervised team are essential. Tellers should have a pleasant personality and good people skills.

A high school diploma is adequate preparation for entry-level jobs, especially if the applicant has had courses in word processing, bookkeeping, office machine operation, and business math.

Banks usually train beginning clerks to operate various office machines. Tellers receive anywhere from a few days to three weeks or more of training and spend some time observing an experienced teller before handling any tasks on their own.

Bank training courses are available to all bank employees throughout their working years. Employees who avail themselves of these courses can advance by gaining new skills. The successful completion of specific banking courses can lead to promotion.

Potential and Advancement

Bank tellers held just under 500,000 jobs in 2000, with about one-fourth working part-time. The great majority worked in commercial banks, savings institutions, or credit unions.

Employment in other positions in banking includes about 85,000 financial managers, 20,000 accountants and auditors, 17,000 credit analysts, 104,000 loan officers, and workers in a variety of other management and support positions.

Total employment in banking is projected to decline 2 percent between 2000 and 2010, compared with the 16 percent growth projected for the economy as a whole. The combined effects of technology, deregulation, mergers, and population increase will continue to affect total employment growth and the mix of occupations in the banking industry. Overall declines in office and administrative support occupations will be offset by gains in professional, managerial, and sales occupations. Although a decline in employment is expected, job opportunities should be plentiful, particularly among tellers and other administrative support staff, who make up a large proportion of bank employees and often transfer to other occupations or leave the labor force.

The banking industry is projected to undergo many changes that will affect employment of traditional tellers. ATMs and the increased use of direct deposit of paychecks and benefit checks, for example, have reduced the need for bank customers to interact with tellers for routine transactions. Electronic banking is spreading rapidly throughout the industry, and this development will reduce the number of tellers over the long run.

Despite the fact that some banks have streamlined their branches, the total number of bank branches is expected to increase to meet the needs of a growing population.

Branches are being added in nontraditional locations, such as grocery stores, malls, and mobile trailers designed to reach people who do not have easy access to banks. These branches are often open longer hours and offer greater customer convenience than do traditional branches. Many of these nontraditional offices are small and are staffed by tellers who also have customer service training. As a result, tellers who can provide a variety of financial services will be in greater demand in the future.

Advances in technology should continue to have the most significant effect on employment in the banking industry. Demand for computer specialists will grow as more banks make their services available electronically and eliminate much of the paperwork involved in many transactions. On the other hand, these changes in technology will reduce the need for several office and administrative support occupations. Other technological improvements, such as digital imaging and computer networking, will adversely affect employment of the "back-office" clerical workers who process checks and other bank statements. Employment of customer service representatives, however, is expected to increase as banks hire more of these workers to staff phone centers and sell banking products to branch customers.

Income

According to the U.S. Department of Labor, average earnings of nonsupervisory bank employees were $417 a week in 2000, compared with $547 for all workers in finance, insurance, and real estate industries, and $474 for workers throughout the private sector. Relatively low salaries in the banking industry reflect the high proportion of low-paying administrative support jobs.

In general, for employees within a given job category, a greater range of responsibilities results in a higher salary. However, experience, length of service, and, especially, the location and size of the bank are also important. Part-time tellers generally do not receive typical benefits, such as life and health insurance.

CITY MANAGER

A city manager administers and coordinates the day-to-day activities of a community and is usually appointed by its elected officials. The city manager oversees such functions as tax collection and disbursement, law enforcement, public works, budget preparation, studies of current problems, and planning for future needs. In a small city, the manager handles all functions; in a larger one, the manager usually has a number of assistants, each of whom manages a department.

City managers and their assistants supervise city employees, coordinate city programs, greet visitors, answer correspondence, prepare reports, represent the city at public hearings and meetings, analyze work procedures, and prepare budgets.

Most city managers work for small cities (population under 25,000) that have a council-manager type of government. The council, which is elected, hires the manager, who is then responsible for running the city as well as for hiring a staff. In cities with a mayor-council type of government, the mayor hires the city manager as his or her top administrative assistant. A few managers work for counties and for metropolitan and regional planning bodies.

Most city managers begin as management assistants in one of the city departments such as finance, public works, or planning. Experience in several different departments is valuable and can provide a well-rounded background. This is a new and growing profession with room for people trained in a variety of disciplines that relate to the functions and problems of urban life.

City managers are employed in cities of all sizes. Working conditions for a city manager are usually those of an office position with considerable public contact. More than forty hours a week is usually required, and emergency situations and public meetings frequently involve evening and weekend work.

Qualifications, Education, and Training

Persons planning a career in city management must be dedicated to public service and willing to work as part of a team. They must have self-confidence, be able to analyze problems and suggest solutions, and should function well under stress. Tact and the ability to communicate well are very important.

A graduate degree is presently required even for most entry-level positions in this field. An undergraduate degree in a discipline such as engineering, recreation, social work, or political science should be followed by a master's degree in public or municipal administration or business administration.

Requirements in some of the colleges and universities that offer advanced degrees in this field include an internship of six months to a year, in which the candidate must work in a city manager's office to gain experience.

Potential and Advancement

Job competition is strong in this field, but it still holds great potential for those with the right qualifications. Increased use of computerized management techniques for taxes, traffic control, and utility billing will create openings for those trained in finance, while increasing emphasis on broad solutions to urban social problems will result in opportunities for those with a strong public administration background. Also, the council-manager system of government is the fastest-growing type in the country, and the trend is toward professional, rather than elected, city management.

Generally, one begins as an assistant to a city manager or department head, with promotions leading to greater responsibility. A city manager will probably work in several different types and sizes of cities over the course of his or her career, which will further broaden the person's experience and promotion potential.

Income

Salaries for city managers depend on education, experience, job responsibility, and the size of the employing city. Salaries are generally high. According to figures published by the U.S. Department of Labor and based on studies conducted by the International Personnel Management Association, city managers earned an average of $92,338 in 2000. County managers averaged $107,500. Benefits usually include travel expenses and a car for official business.

COMPUTER PROGRAMMER

Computer programmers write detailed instructions, called programs, that list the orderly steps a computer must follow to solve a problem. Once programming is completed, the programmer runs a sample of the data to make sure the program is correct and will produce the desired information. This is called "debugging." If there are any errors, the program must be changed and rechecked until it produces the correct results. The final step is the preparation of an instruction sheet for the computer operator who will be running the program.

A simple program can be written and debugged in a few days. Those that use many data files or complex mathematical formulas may require a year or more of work. On such large projects, several programmers work together under the supervision of an experienced programmer.

Programmers usually work from problem descriptions prepared by systems analysts who have examined the problem and determined the next steps necessary to solve it. In organizations that do not employ systems analysts, employees known as programmer-analysts handle both functions. An applications programmer then writes detailed instructions for programming the data. Applications programmers usually specialize in business or scientific work. A systems programmer is a specialist who maintains the general instructions (software) that control the operation of the entire computer system.

Most programmers are employed by manufacturing firms, banks, insurance companies, data processing services, utilities, and government agencies. Systems programmers usually work in research organizations, computer manufacturing firms, and large computer centers.

Computer programmers are employed in virtually all areas of North America. Most work a forty-hour week, but their hours are not always nine to five. They may occasionally work on weekends or at other odd hours to have access to the computer when it is not needed for scheduled work.

Qualifications, Education, and Training

Patience, persistence, and accuracy are necessary characteristics for a programmer. Ingenuity, imagination, and the ability to think logically are also important. High school experience should include as many mathematics and computer courses as possible.

Many computer programmers have a bachelor's or more advanced degree. Typical majors include computer science, mathematics, and information systems. Other programmers hold associate degrees in similar areas.

Computer programming courses are offered by vocational and technical schools, colleges and universities, and community colleges. Online and home-study courses are also available, and a few high schools offer some training in programming.

Scientific organizations require college training; some require advanced degrees in computer science, mathematics, engineering, or the physical sciences.

Because of rapidly changing technologies, programmers take periodic training courses offered by employers, software vendors, and computer manufacturers. Like physicians, they must keep constantly abreast of the latest developments in their field. These courses also aid in advancement and promotion.

Potential and Advancement

The Department of Labor predicts that employment of programmers will grow about as fast as the average for all occupations through 2010. Jobs for both systems and applications programmers should be most plentiful in data processing service firms, software houses, and computer consulting businesses. These types of establishments are part of computer and data processing services, which is projected to be the fastest-growing industry overall through 2010.

As businesses and nonprofit organizations attempt to control costs and keep up with changing technology, they will need programmers to assist in conversions to new computer languages and systems. In addition, many job openings will result from the need to replace programmers who leave the labor force or transfer to other occupations such as manager or systems analyst.

There are many opportunities for advancement in this field. In large organizations, programmers may be promoted to jobs with supervisory responsibilities. Both applications programmers and systems programmers can be promoted to systems analyst positions.

Income

Median annual earnings of computer programmers were $57,590 in 2000, according to the U.S. Department of Labor. The middle 50 percent earned between $44,850 and $74,500 a year. The lowest 10 percent earned less than $35,020; the highest 10 percent earned more than $93,210.

According to studies by Robert Half International as reported by the DOL, average annual starting salaries in 2001 ranged from $58,500 to $90,000 for applications development programmers/developers, and from $54,000 to $77,750 for software development programmers/analysts. Average starting salaries for Internet programmers/analysts ranged from $56,500 to $84,000.

INVESTMENT MANAGER

An investment manager's function is to manage a company's or an institution's investments. Investment decisions involve such matters as what to buy in the way of securities, property for investment, or other items; or when to sell existing holdings for maximum return on investment.

Also called financial analysts and securities analysts, these investment specialists work for banks (where they are usually officers), insurance companies, brokerage firms, and pension plan investment firms and mutual funds. They may function as trustees for institutions or individuals with large holdings or for colleges that have endowment funds to manage. Some use their expertise as financial journalists, analyzing the market for financial publications, newspapers, and magazines. (For a detailed description of the tasks of people involved in this field, see the job description for market analyst next in this chapter.)

Investment managers work in all parts of the United States and Canada, but are concentrated in large cities such as Boston, Chicago, New York City, Toronto, and San Francisco.

The work is very time consuming since investment specialists must read constantly—newspapers, annual reports, trade publications—to keep abreast of developments and changes in the market.

Qualifications, Education, and Training

Facility in mathematics; ability to digest, analyze, and interpret large amounts of material; an inquiring mind; and good communication skills are important in this field.

A college degree in economics, political science, business administration, finance, or marketing is preferred in the investment arena. Engineering or law, especially if combined with graduate work in business administration, can also provide an excellent background. Training in mathematics, statistics, and computers is becoming increasingly important.

The mark of professionalism in this field is the chartered financial analyst (CFA) certificate, which is comparable to the certified public accountant (CPA) for an accountant. To earn it, the applicant must fulfill the membership requirements of one of the financial analyst societies and complete three examination programs. Five or more years of experience as a financial analyst are required before the third examination can be taken.

Potential and Advancement

Job opportunities will be good in the foreseeable future for those with the appropriate degrees and experience. Since this is already a high-level position in most organizations, further advancement for an investment manager usually takes the form of moving to a larger institution or organization, if the individual has achieved a reputation for accurate analysis and wise management of investments.

Income

Investment managers who work in banking or for large institutions, such as colleges, earn up to $75,000 or more a year. Salaries for top-level analysts in this field vary widely. Some with excellent reputations earn well over $100,000 per year.

MARKET ANALYST

The decision to buy, hold, or sell securities is sometimes made by utilizing the knowledge of the individual buyer or seller, but most investors consult their stockbrokers for advice. The stockbroker, in turn, depends on the expertise of the research department of his firm to provide the necessary information. These experts are called market analysts or securities analysts.

In addition to working in brokerage houses, market analysts and securities analysts are also employed by investment banking firms, bank trust departments, insurance companies, pension and mutual funds, investment advisory firms, and institutions such as colleges that have endowment funds to manage. All these organizations expect the same thing: expert advice that will help them to invest wisely with the best return on their money.

Market analysts evaluate the market as a whole. They study information on changes in the gross national product, cost of living, personal income, rate of employment, construction starts, fiscal plans of the federal government, growth and inflation rates, balance of payments, market trends, and indexes of common stocks. They also monitor events that might produce a psychological reaction in the market: international crises, political activity, or a tragedy large enough to cause the market to change direction. Market analysts also keep an eye on business and industry developments and the actions of the Federal Reserve to loosen or tighten credit.

Securities analysts study and analyze individual companies or industries, relating knowledge of the current and future state of the economy to predict the future performance of the company or industry in question. Analysts may specialize in a particular area, such as firms involved in energy production or the aircraft-manufacturing industry. The analyst studies all available material on an individual company, including annual reports and details of company management, and sometimes visits the business to take a closer look in person.

An investor with an investment portfolio containing a number of different securities needs advice not only on the individual securities but also on the makeup of the entire portfolio. A portfolio analyst has the broad general knowledge to give advice on the market and its relationship to the investor's objectives. The accumulation of a balanced portfolio can then be accomplished.

Those analysts who deal in securities actually combine elements of all of these three areas within the scope of their work. But in organizations that employ large numbers of researchers, the jobs are often separate. Related jobs are actuary, economist, insurance agent and broker, investment manager, statistician, securities sales worker, and stockbroker.

Analysts work in all parts of North America but are concentrated in large cities such as Boston, Chicago, New York City, and San Francisco. Major brokerage houses have branch offices in about eight hundred cities.

Analysts find their work fascinating but time consuming. They must read constantly—newspapers, annual reports, trade publications—to keep abreast of developments and changes in the market. Their advancement depends on the reputation they achieve for accurate analysis and predictions. They are sometimes required to make decisions quickly about securities worth thousands, or even millions, of dollars.

Qualifications, Education, and Training

The ability to interpret and analyze large amounts of material, an inquiring mind, and facility in mathematics are absolutely necessary. Good communications skills are also important.

A college degree is required by just about all employers. Economics, political science, and business administration are the preferred degrees. Engineering, law, finance, and marketing, especially when combined with graduate work in business administration, are also accepted. The growing use of computers in this field often requires the addition to research staffs of those trained in mathematics and statistics.

The mark of professionalism among analysts is the chartered financial analyst (CFA) degree, comparable to the CPA for an accountant. To earn this degree, an analyst must fulfill the membership requirements of one of the financial analyst societies in the United States and complete three examination programs. Analysts must have five or more years of experience before taking the third examination.

Potential and Advancement

Government projections are that increased investment by businesses and individuals will result in faster-than-average employment growth of financial analysts through 2010. This occupation will benefit as baby boomers save for retirement and a generally better educated and wealthier population requires investment advice. As the number of mutual funds and the amount of assets invested in the funds increases, mutual fund companies will need more financial analysts to recommend which financial products the funds should buy or sell.

Growth in retirement plans will also increase demand for personal financial advisers to provide guidance on how to invest this money. Deregulation of the financial services industry is also expected to spur demand for financial analysts and personal financial advisers. Since 1999, banks, insurance companies, and brokerage firms have been allowed to broaden their financial services. Many firms are adding investment advice to their list of offerings and are expected to increase their hiring of personal financial advisers. Numerous banks are now entering the securities brokerage and investment banking fields and will increasingly need the skills of financial analysts in these areas.

The globalization of the securities markets as well as the increased complexity of many financial products also will increase the need for analysts and advisers to help investors make financial choices. In addition, business mergers and acquisitions seem likely to continue, requiring the services of financial analysts. In the field of investment banking, however, the demand for financial analysts may fluctuate because investment banking is sensitive to changes in the stock market. Further consolidation in the financial services industry may eliminate some financial analyst positions, some-what dampening overall employment growth. Competition is expected to be keen for these highly lucrative positions, with many more applicants than jobs.

Income

According to the U.S. Department of Labor, median annual earnings of financial analysts were $52,420 in 2000. The middle half earned between $40,210 and $70,840. The lowest 10 percent earned less than $31,880, and the top 10 percent earned more than $101,760.

Median annual earnings in the industries employing the largest numbers of financial analysts in 2000 were:

Security and commodity services	$65,920
Security brokers and dealers	$54,650
Management and public relations	$52,690
Computer and data processing services	$51,680
Commercial banks	$46,910

Financial analysts may receive bonuses in addition to their salaries, which can add substantially to their earnings. The bonus is usually based on how well their predictions compare to the actual performance of a benchmark investment.

CHAPTER

8

DESIGNING A WINNING RÉSUMÉ

Once you have acquired the qualities and skills that financial services companies seek in potential employees, you must sell yourself to prospective employers. This means not only finding the jobs for which you want to apply, but presenting yourself in the best way possible.

JOB SEARCH STRATEGIES

There are many ways to find job leads and research potential employers at the same time. Contact financial services associations in your area to see which ones have student chapters or offer student memberships. A list of some professional associations and organizations can be found in Appendix A. You can find even more at your local public or university library. These associations also may be a source of job listings or literature explaining the general employment outlook in the field.

It's always a good idea to keep up on the latest business news. Excellent sources of general business and finance news include the *Wall Street Journal, Barron's, BusinessWeek, Forbes, Fortune, Inc.,* and *Financial World.* In addition, there are many highly specialized financial publications, such as *American Banker, Investment Dealers Digest,* and *Institutional Investor.* Regional business publications and the business sections of major metropolitan newspapers can provide further perspective. A number of these publications carry recruitment advertising as well; many also operate informative websites. The U.S. Department of Labor's *Occupational Outlook Handbook*, available at library reference departments and online at www.bls.gov, gives a picture of employment trends in various fields.

College placement departments or career services offices assist graduating students in obtaining positions, but their services extend beyond that, and students should not wait until senior year to find out about them. Placement directors often are able to suggest summer employment possibilities and offer assistance with career decisions, including suggestions concerning recommended classes to meet requirements for positions in which a student expresses interest.

Each year, companies send representatives to college campuses to interview seniors seeking employment after graduation. The placement director and the department staff are responsible for arranging interviews. Recruiters usually bring with them literature describing the company's policies for hiring and promotion, and other information about the firm or government agency. College placement departments keep a supply of these brochures on hand for students who want to research companies before being interviewed. Students who "do their homework" can ask better questions and obtain more information from interviewers than those who enter an interview "cold." Furthermore, they will be more effective during the interviews and be better able to make sound employment decisions.

DESIGNING AN EFFECTIVE RÉSUMÉ

Résumés provide employers with written evidence of your qualifications and skills. A winning résumé is made up of the elements that employers are most interested in seeing when reviewing a job applicant. These basic elements are the ingredients of a successful résumé and are essential. The following list of elements may be used in a résumé. Some are essential, some are optional; we will discuss these further to give you a better understanding of each element's role in the makeup of your résumé:

- Heading
- Objective
- Work experience

- Education
- Honors
- Activities
- Certificates and licenses
- Professional memberships
- Special skills
- References

Gathering Information

The first step in preparing your résumé is to gather together all the information about yourself and your past accomplishments. Later you will refine this information, rewrite it in the most effective language, and organize it into the most attractive layout. First, let's take a look at each of these important elements individually.

Heading

The heading may seem a simple enough element in your résumé, but take care not to treat it lightly. The heading should be placed at the top of your résumé and should include your name, home address, and telephone numbers. If you can take calls at your current place of business, include your work number, since most employers will attempt to contact you during the business day. Always include your phone number on your résumé. It is crucial for prospective employers to have immediate contact with you when necessary.

Objective

When seeking a particular career path, you may want to list a job objective on your résumé (although some experts now say this is not necessary). If you choose to include an objective, use it to help an employer understand the direction you wish to go, so that he or she can determine whether your goals are in line with the position available. The objective is normally one sentence long and describes your employment goals clearly and concisely.

The job objective will vary depending on the type of person you are and the kind of goals you have. It can be either specific or general, but it should always be to the point.

Work Experience

This element is arguably the most important of them all. It provides the central focus of your résumé, so this section must be as complete as possible. Only by examining your work experience in depth can you reach the heart of your accomplishments and present them in a way that demonstrates the strength of your qualifications. Of course, a recent graduate will have less work experience than someone who has been working for a number of years, but the amount of information isn't the most important thing—rather, how it is presented and how it highlights you as a person and as a worker.

As you complete this section of your résumé, be aware of the need for accuracy. You'll want to include all necessary information about each of your jobs, including job title, dates, employer, city, and state, responsibilities, special projects, and accomplishments. Be sure to list only company accomplishments for which you were directly responsible. If you haven't participated in any special projects, that's all right—this area may not be relevant to certain jobs.

A basic rule of résumé writing, and an extremely important one, is to list all work experience in reverse chronological order. In other words, always start with your most recent job and work your way backward. This way your prospective employer sees your current (and usually most important) job before seeing your less critical past jobs. Your most recent position should also be the one that includes the most information as compared to your previous ones. If you are just out of school, show your summer employment and part-time work, though your education will most likely be more important than your experience in this case.

Education

Education is the second most important element of a résumé. Your educational background is often a crucial factor in an employer's decision to hire you. Be sure to stress your accomplishments in school with the same finesse that you described your accomplishments at work. If you are looking for your first job, your education will be your greatest asset, since your work experience will most likely be minimal. In this case, the education section becomes the most important. Be sure to include any degrees or certificates you received, your major area of concentration, any honors, and any relevant activities. Again, be sure to list your most recent schooling first.

Honors

List any awards, honors, or memberships in honorary societies that you have received. These are usually of an academic nature, but they can also be for special achievement in sports, clubs, or other school activities. Always be sure to include the name of the organization honoring you and the date(s) received; for example, Dean's List, 2003 or Phi Beta Kappa, 2004.

Activities

You may have been active in different organizations or clubs during your years at school, and often an employer will look at such involvement as evidence of initiative and dedication. Your ability to take an active and even a leadership role in a group should be included on your résumé.

Certificates and Licenses

The next potential element of your résumé is certificates and licenses. You should list these if the job you are seeking requires them and you, of course, have acquired them. If you have applied for a license but have not yet received it, use the phrase "application pending."

Always be sure that all of the information you list is completely accurate. Locate copies of your licenses and certificates and check the exact date and name of the accrediting agency; for example, Teaching Certificate, State of Illinois Board of Education, 2004.

Professional Memberships

List any involvement in professional associations, unions, and similar organizations. It is to your advantage to record any professional memberships that pertain to the job you are seeking. Be sure to include the dates of your participation and whether you took part in any special activities or held any offices within the organization; for example, United Garment Workers Association, Secretary/Treasurer, 2002–2004.

Special Skills

This section of your résumé is set aside for mentioning any special abilities you have that could relate to the job you are seeking. Today, virtually all employers look for applicants who have computer experience. Be sure to list all types of computer hardware and software with which you are familiar.

Knowledge of a particular type of software is sometimes essential if the company interviewing you uses it exclusively. This is the part of your résumé where you can display certain talents and experiences that are not necessarily part of your education or work.

Another beneficial special skill is knowledge of a foreign language. Open a newspaper to the classified section and you will notice numerous job openings for those with bilingual skills. Be sure to disclose if you are fluent or simply have a working knowledge of the language; this will make a difference to your employer.

Special skills can encompass a wide range of talents—from being a free-lance editor to being an expert photographer. Just make sure that whatever skills you list relate directly or indirectly to the type of work for which you are looking.

References

References are not usually listed on one's résumé, but a prospective employer needs to know that you have references and that they may be contacted if necessary. All you need to include on your résumé is a sentence at the bottom of the résumé stating, "References available on request." Forewarn all of your references that they may receive a call about you; then they will be prepared to give you the best reference possible.

Writing It Out

Now that you have gathered together all of the information for each section, it's time to write out each part of your résumé in a way that will get the attention of the person reviewing it. The type of language you use in your résumé has a profound effect on its success. You want to take the information you have gathered and translate it into a language that will make a potential employer sit up and take notice.

Résumé writing is not like expository writing or creative writing. It embodies a functional, direct style and focuses on the use of action words or verbs. By using action words in your writing, you stress more effectively past accomplishments. Action words help demonstrate your initiative and highlight your talents. Always use verbs that show strength and reflect the qualities of a "doer." For example, instead of "Put together a sales plan for the Midwest," use "Orchestrated a regional sales plan that increased sales in several midwestern states." Instead of "The newspaper was redesigned while I was managing editor," say "Served as managing editor. Redesigned newspaper's layout." By using action words, you characterize yourself as a person who takes action, and this will impress potential employers.

Assembling the Elements

At this point, you've gathered all the necessary information for your résumé, and you've rewritten this information using language that will impress potential employers. Your next step is to assemble these elements into a logical order and then to set them on the page neatly and attractively to achieve the desired result: getting that interview.

Assembly

The order of the elements of a résumé makes a difference in its overall effect. You would obviously not want to put your name and address in the middle of the résumé or your special skills section at the top. You need to put the elements in an order that stresses your most important achievements, not less pertinent information. For example, if you are a recent graduate and have no full-time work experience, you should list your education before you list any part-time jobs you may have held while attending school. On the other hand, if you have been gainfully employed for several years and currently hold an important position in your company, you should list your work experience ahead of your education, which has become less pertinent with time.

There are some elements that are always included in a résumé, and some that are optional. The following is a list of essential and optional elements:

Essential	*Optional*
Name	Job objective
Address	Honors
Phone number	Special skills
Work experience	Professional memberships
Education	Activities
References	Certificates and licenses

Your choice to include optional sections depends on your own background and employment needs. Always use information that will put you and your abilities in a favorable light. If your honors are impressive, be sure to include them on your résumé. If your school activities demonstrate particular talents advantageous for the job you are seeking, allow space for a section on activities. Each résumé is as unique as the person it describes.

Types of Résumés

So far, our discussion has focused on the most common type of résumé—the reverse chronological résumé. This is the type usually preferred by human resources directors, and it is the one most frequently used. In some cases, however, this style of presentation is not the most effective way to highlight one's skills and accomplishments.

For someone re-entering the workforce after many years or looking to change career fields, the functional résumé may work best. This type of résumé focuses more on achievement and less on the sequence of your work history. In the functional résumé, your experience is presented by what you have accomplished and the skills you have developed in your past work.

A functional résumé can be assembled from the same information you collected for your chronological résumé. The main difference lies in how you use this information. Essentially, the work experience portion becomes two sections, with your job duties and accomplishments comprising one section and your employer's name, and city, and state, your position, and the dates employed making up another section. The first section is placed near the top of the résumé, just below the job objective, and can be called "Accomplishments" or "Achievements." The second section, containing the bare essentials of your employment history, should follow the accomplishments section and can be titled "Work Experience" or "Employment History." The other sections of your résumé remain the same; the work experience section is the only one affected in the functional résumé. By placing the section that focuses on your achievements first, you draw attention to these achievements. This puts less emphasis on who you worked for and more emphasis on what you did and what you are capable of doing.

For someone changing careers, emphasis on skills and achievements is essential. The identities of previous employers, which may be unrelated to one's new job field, should be downplayed. The functional résumé accomplishes this task. For someone reentering the workforce after many years, a functional résumé is the obvious choice. If you lack full-time work experience, you need to draw attention away from this fact and instead focus on the skills and abilities gained through volunteer activities or part-time work. Education may also play a more important role in this résumé.

The type of résumé that is right for you depends on your own personal circumstances. It may be helpful to create both a chronological and a functional résumé and then compare the two to assess which is more suitable. The sample résumés found in this book include both chronological and functional résumés. Use these as guides to help you decide on the content and appearance of your own résumé. Exhibit 8.1 is an example of a chronological résumé; an example of a functional résumé is shown in Exhibit 8.2.

Layout

Once you have decided which elements to include and you have arranged them in an order that makes sense and emphasizes your achievements and abilities, it is time to work on the physical layout of your résumé.

There is no single appropriate layout that applies to every résumé, but there are a few basic rules to follow in putting your résumé on paper.

1. Leave a comfortable margin at the sides, top, and bottom of the page (usually 1 to 1½ inches). You may need to reduce the size of the margins in order to fit your résumé on one page, however.
2. Use appropriate spacing between the sections (usually 2 to 3 line spaces are adequate).
3. Be consistent in the type of headings used for the different sections of your résumé. For example, if you capitalize the heading WORK EXPERIENCE, don't use initial capitals and underlining for a heading of equal importance, such as Education.
4. Try to fit your résumé onto one page, if possible. Don't let the idea of telling every detail about your life get in the way of producing a résumé that is simple and straightforward. The more compact your résumé, the easier it will be to read and the better impression it will make for you.

Try experimenting with various layouts until you find one that looks good. It may be helpful to show your final layout to others and get their opinions. Ask them what impresses them most about your résumé. Make sure this is what you want most to emphasize. If it isn't, consider making changes in your layout until the necessary information is stressed. Use the sample résumés on the following pages (see Exhibits 8.3 to 8.6) to get some ideas for laying out your résumé. (See also Appendix B.)

Proofreading

Before you have your résumé copied or printed, you must thoroughly check it for typing and spelling errors. Have several people read it over just in case you have missed something. Misspelled words and typing mistakes will not make a good impression on a prospective employer; they reflect poorly on your writing ability and attention to detail. With thorough and conscientious proofreading, these mistakes can be avoided.

Exhibit 8.1 Chronological Résumé

Andrew M. Thomas

3663 N. Coldwater Canyon   (818) 555-3472   athomas@blank.com
Los Angeles, CA 90390   (818) 555-3678

JOB OBJECTIVE: A position as a sales/marketing manager where I can utilize my knowledge and experience by combining high-volume selling of major accounts with an administrative ability that increases sales through encouragement of sales team.

EMPLOYMENT HISTORY: Tribor Industries, Los Angeles, CA
Regional Sales Manager, 2003–present
Managed sales of all product lines in western markets for a leading maker of linens. Represented five corporate divisions of the company with sales in excess of $3,000,000 annually. Directed and motivated a sales force of twelve sales representatives in planned selling to achieve company goals.

Tribor Industries, Los Angeles, CA
District Manager, 1998–2003
Acted as sales representative for the Los Angeles metropolitan area. Built both wholesale and dealer distribution substantially during my tenure. Promoted to regional sales manager after five years' service.

American Office Supply, Chicago, IL
Assistant to Sales Manager, 1991–1998
Handled both internal and external areas of sales and marketing, including samples, advertising, and pricing. Served as company sales representative and sold a variety of office supplies to retail stores.

EDUCATION: University of Michigan, Ann Arbor, MI
BA Business Administration, 1991
Major Field: Management

SEMINARS: National Management Association Seminars, 1996, 2002
Purdue University Seminars, 1993, 2004

PROFESSIONAL MEMBERSHIPS: Sales and Marketing Association of Los Angeles
National Association of Market Developers

REFERENCES: Available on request

Exhibit 8.2 Functional Résumé

Regina Ford

1532 Walnut Street, Sacramento, CA 95819   (916) 555-3663   fordfamily@blank.net

OBJECTIVE: A supervisory position that utilizes my experience and skills to generate staff effectiveness, enhance productivity, and meet organizational goals.

SUMMARY OF QUALIFICATIONS

- Sixteen years experience in retail banking and five years in operations.
- Skilled at team building, creative problem solving, and technical training.
- Communicate well with senior management, staff, and customers.

ANALYSIS OF EXPERIENCE

Supervision

- Monitored daily workload.
- Hired and trained staff.
- Established policies for handling customer complaints to promote quality service and quick resolution.
- Prepared monthly management reports.
- Developed employee incentive program.
- Introduced ideas that reduced expenses by 25 percent.

Customer Service

- Directed staff of ten customer service representatives.
- Settled payment disputes.
- Answered numerous phone calls and letters daily.
- Redesigned job functions to improve quality control standards.
- Cross-trained staff in several positions to cover for vacations and absences.

Accounting

- Reconciled outstanding items on bank statements.
- Cleared and reconciled bank advices.
- Established new depository account procedures.

WORK EXPERIENCE

Customer Service Supervisor, First National Bank, Sacramento, CA, 2001 to present
Branch Service Manager, Wells Fargo, Modesto, CA, and Merced, CA, 1993–2001
Operations Supervisor, Wells Fargo, Stockton, CA, 1988–1993

EDUCATION

California State University, Sacramento, CA
BA, Business Management, 1987
Several American Institute of Banking courses

PERSONAL INTERESTS

Bowling, hiking, softball, and reading

Exhibit 8.3 Sample Résumé

Adam Jones

1501 N. Polk Avenue   Springfield, IL 66660   (217) 555-5552   aj24@blank.com

POSITION DESIRED: Financial Management Director

SKILLS and ACHIEVEMENTS

Research
- Conducted consumer surveys.
- Coordinated policy formulation.
- Developed advertising concepts and strategies.
- Controlled transportation and distribution costs.

Development
- Handled cost forecasting and pricing policies.
- Implemented costing techniques.
- Oversaw research and development budgeting.
- Conducted feasibility studies.

Planning
- Handled long- and short-range financial forecasting.
- Managed capital investment opportunities.
- Made financial projections.
- Directed tax reductions and budgets.

Analysis
- Involved in statistical methodologies and analysis.
- Administered trend analysis.
- Conducted media evaluations and survey designs.

WORK EXPERIENCE

Control Data, Inc., Springfield, IL
Senior Financial Analyst, 1997–present
Warner Co., Jackson, MS
Financial Analyst, 1987–97

EDUCATION

Howard University, Washington, D.C.,
  MA in Financial Planning, 1987
Thelonious College, Jackson, MS
  BA in Economics, 1985

Exhibit 8.4 Sample Résumé

G. Isaac Schwabacher

310 East 80th Street, #201   (212) 555-6351 (W)   isaacs@blank.net
New York, NY 10028   (212) 555-4189 (H)

PROFESSIONAL EXPERIENCE

Tax Manager, Deloitte & Touche, New York, NY,
December 2000–Present

- Tax planning and research for entertainment, retail sales,
  and leasing firms.
  Perform due diligence analysis and financial planning on
  mergers and acquisitions.
- Supervise preparation of partnership and corporate tax returns. Review tax provisions for clients.
  Hire and train
  professional staff.

Tax Manager, Coopers & Lybrand, Albany, NY,
September 1996–December 2000

AFFILIATIONS

Licensed to practice law in New York
Member, Tax Section, American Bar Association
Member, United Jewish Fund
Volunteer, Business Volunteers for the Arts

EDUCATION

JD, Columbia University Law School, New York, NY, 1996
BA, Economics, Duke University, Durham, NC, 1992

Exhibit 8.5 Sample Résumé

Robin J. Lawford
68 Lake Street   (313) 555-7426   polo99@blank.com
Ann Arbor, MI 48109

OBJECTIVE
Position in investment banking.

PROFESSIONAL EXPERIENCE
Summer 2004

Associate—Investment Banking, Morgan Stanley, Chicago, IL
- Analyzed debt, equity, and derivative products for telecommunications clients.
- Worked on merger and acquisition presentation for a European client.
- Assisted in due diligence for a major industrial company's IPO.

2000–2003

Analyst—Planning and Analysis, Cygnet Insurance Company, Paris, France
- Drafted annual business plans and revenue and profit projections.
- Analyzed variances from fiscal plan.
- Prepared monthly financial statements for internal use.
- Developed an MIS mainframe application.

EDUCATION
MBA, Finance and Communications, University of Michigan School of Business, 2004
BA, English, Dartmouth University 2000
Exchange Program, The Sorbonne, Paris, France, 1998

ADDITIONAL INFORMATION
Member: International Business Club and Women in Banking Association
Fluent in French and German
Traveled extensively in Europe
Enjoy painting, water polo, and tennis

Exhibit 8.6 Sample Résumé

Peter Thomasson

Fulton Hall   312/555-4849   prt@xxx.net

2300 East Harrison, Room 306

Chicago, IL 60633

OBJECTIVE

A career in the field of finance.

EDUCATION

University of Illinois at Chicago, Chicago, IL

Bachelor of Arts in Economics

Expected June 2006

HONORS

Phi Beta Kappa

Dean's list five times

Robeson Business Scholarship, 2004

ACTIVITIES

Vice President, Beta Gamma Fraternity

Freshman Adviser

Homecoming Planning Committee

Baseball Team

Student Rights Group

WORK EXPERIENCE

IBM, Northbrook, IL

Accounting Intern, 2003

Assisted finance department in the areas of computer accounting, bookkeeping, financial
statements, forecasts, and planning. Extensive use of spreadsheet software programs.

University of Illinois at Chicago

Office Assistant, Journalism School, 2002–2004

Assisted with registrations, filing, and typing

Arranged application materials, assembled course packs

General Office, Registrar, 2002

Processed transcript requests. Entered registrations on the computer.

Provided informational assistance to students.

SPECIAL SKILLS

Hands-on computer experience using a variety of software packages in database management.

CHAPTER

9

COMPOSING AN EFFECTIVE COVER LETTER

The purpose of the cover letter is to get a potential employer to read your résumé, just as the purpose of your résumé is to get that same potential employer to call you for an interview.

Once your résumé has been assembled, laid out, and printed to your satisfaction, the next and final step before distribution is to write your cover letter. Most often you will be sending your résumé via E-mail, and it must always be accompanied by a letter that briefly introduces you and your résumé.

Like your résumé, your cover letter should be clean, neat, and direct. A cover letter usually includes the following information:

- Your name, address, and E-mail address, if you choose to include the latter (unless this information already appears on your personal letterhead).
- The date.
- The name and address of the person and company to whom you are sending your résumé.
- The salutation ("Dear Mr." or "Dear Ms." followed by the person's last name, or "To Whom It May Concern" if you are answering a blind ad).
- An opening paragraph explaining why you are writing (in response to an ad, as the result of a previous meeting, or at the suggestion of someone you both know) and indicating that you are interested in whatever job is being offered.

- One or two more paragraphs that tell why you want to work for the company and what qualifications and experience you can bring to the firm.
- A final paragraph that closes the letter and requests that you be contacted for an interview.
- The closing ("Sincerely," or "Yours Truly," followed by your signature with your name typed under it).

Your cover letter, including all of the above information, should be no more than one page in length. The language used should be polite, businesslike, and to the point. Do not attempt to tell your life story in the cover letter. A long and cluttered missive will only serve to put off the reader. Remember, you only need to mention a few of your accomplishments and skills in the cover letter. The rest of your information is in your résumé. Each and every achievement does not need to be mentioned twice. If your cover letter is a success, your résumé will be read and all pertinent information reviewed by your prospective employer.

PRODUCING THE COVER LETTER

Cover letters should always be produced individually, since they are always written to particular individuals and companies. Never use a form letter for your cover letter. Cover letters cannot be copied or reproduced like résumés. Each one should be as personal as possible. Of course, once you have written and rewritten your first cover letter to the point where you are satisfied with it, you certainly can use similar wording in subsequent letters.

After you have composed your cover letter, be sure to proofread it as thoroughly as you did your résumé. Again, spelling errors are a sure sign of carelessness, and you don't want that to be part of your first impression on a prospective employer. Be sure to keep an accurate record of all the résumés you send out and the results of each mailing.

Some sample cover letters appear on the following pages (Exhibits 9.1 to 9.5). Use them as models for your own cover letter or to get an idea of how cover letters are put together. Remember, each one is unique and depends on the particular circumstances of the individual writing it.

Exhibit 9.1 Sample Cover Letter

113
Composing an
Effective Cover Letter

MARTIN CHANG • 964 N. Tenth Street • Springfield, IL 62713 • (217) 555-5240 • chang66@blank.net

Mr. Jeff Franklin   October 15, 2004
Human Resources
Bethlehem Steel
4000 Hammond Road
Gary, IN 46634

Dear Mr. Franklin:

I would greatly appreciate the opportunity to talk to you about your firm's need for a financial analyst. The position you offered in the October 14 advertisement in the Chicago Tribune interests me because it would enable me to utilize my analytical skills in a basic industry.

My education and work experience have certainly prepared me to contribute to Bethlehem Steel. My course work in economics and my position as senior financial analyst with the Illinois Department of Commerce have honed my quantitative and analytical skills. Furthermore, I am well acquainted with the steel industry as I have represented the state of Illinois in its economic development efforts targeting the steel industry. I am confident that these qualifications will be assets in a position as a financial analyst with your firm.

I appreciate your time and consideration. I hope to have a chance to talk to you about the advertised position.

Sincerely,

Martin Chang (signature)

Martin Chang

Enc. Résumé

Exhibit 9.2 Sample Cover Letter

Geraldine Powers   April 5, 2004
Powers & Powers, Inc.
7700 Main Street
Las Vegas, NV 88883

Dear Ms. Powers:

After spending the last two years as an accountant for Hervey &
Co., I feel that I am ready to pursue a management position in a
larger accounting firm such as yours. Powers & Powers' reputation as
a leader in the field has led me to write to you regarding possible
management opportunities in your company.

At Hervey & Co., I have managed insurance, financial, and brokerage accounting, handled general cost accounting procedures, and
designed systems for budget and cash flow accounting. During these
past two years, I have developed solid accounting skills. Now I feel
that I am ready for something more challenging.

I am enclosing my résumé for your perusal. Please contact me
regarding any openings appropriate for me.

Sincerely,

Crystal Cartier (signature)

Crystal Cartier
1201 E. Maple Drive
Las Vegas, NV 89901

Exhibit 9.3 Sample Cover Letter

115
Composing an
Effective Cover Letter

CARLOS RODRIGUEZ • **68 Via Robles Drive** • **Valencia, CA 91355** • **(805) 555-6050**

Mr. Nick Ponti   October 3, 2004
President
Community Bank of Coral Gables
200 Main Street
Coral Gables, FL 33114

Dear Mr. Ponti:

Are you getting the maximum results possible from your commercial lending activities? Have you penetrated the sought-after middle market? If not, my background may be of interest to you. My extensive commercial lending experience includes exposure in credit analysis, investments, and planning. I am particularly skilled at developing and retaining customer relations through innovative professional service.

During the past twenty-five years, I have held management positions of increasing responsibility covering all aspects of commercial lending. As an analytical and enthusiastic problem solver, I can provide your bank with the experience necessary to achieve an improved bottom line.

The following are a few of my major accomplishments that may interest your organization:

* Established a $40 million industrial and commercial loan portfolio that achieved consistent returns.
* Designed new security and foreign exchange trading activities. Assisted a major foreign bank in opening operations in California.
* Produced a 25 percent return on equity with the account officer concept.

I have earned a B.A. in economics from the University of Madrid, Spain. I speak fluent Spanish, which should be an asset in Coral Gables. I am sure that I could make the kind of forward-thinking, growth-oriented contributions your bank would require. I have only presented a brief summary of my qualifications and accomplishments and therefore would like to meet with you to discuss ways in which my extensive background could make a major contribution to your bank.

Sincerely,

Carlos Rodriguez (signature)

Carlos Rodriguez

Enclosure: Résumé

Exhibit 9.4 Sample Cover Letter

Harvard Peter Fendi   September 25, 2004
President
American Finance Co.
4444 E. River Drive
Detroit, MI 33393

Dear Mr. Fendi:

As a recent graduate of the Kellogg School of Business Management at Northwestern University, I am seeking a position in financial management. I met a representative of your company, Jonathon Siveva, at a recruiting seminar at Northwestern a few months ago, and he alerted me to the fact that your company would be hiring MBAs this summer. Hence, this letter.

At Kellogg, my concentration was in finance. I was in the Finance Club and served as a member of the Student Advisory Board. My practical experience includes a financial accounting internship at Thomas & Thomas, an internship in the commercial loan department at LaSalle National Bank, and a position in the accounts payable department at Northwestern.

I am enclosing my résumé for a more comprehensive picture of my accomplishments and qualifications. I will contact you in the next ten days to inquire about setting up an interview. Please feel free to contact me at the number listed below.

Sincerely,

Antonio Marino (signature)

Antonio Marino
8900 Lake Shore Drive, #442
Chicago, IL 60614
(312) 555-2939
apmarino@blank.net

Exhibit 9.5 Sample Cover Letter

117
Composing an
Effective Cover Letter

Carlos Castillo   October 7, 2004
Director of Human Resources
Macy's, Inc.
5744 N. Franklin Avenue
Miami, FL 33333

Dear Mr. Castillo:

I am responding to your advertisement for a Senior Audit Manager
for your company. The ad requested someone with audit experience
in a department store. I have such experience.

For the past six years, I have served as Audit Manager for Jordan
Marsh Co. in Ft. Myers, FL. My responsibilities include overseeing
analytical review and verification of financial records, developing
audit programs, and establishing guidelines for physical distribution
and evaluation of internal controls. Before Jordan Marsh, I worked
for National Textile Co., and Held & Perkins, both in the area of audit
and finance.

My résumé is enclosed in order to give you a complete picture of
my experience and qualifications. Please review it and contact me if
you would like me to come for an interview. I look forward to hearing
from you soon.

Sincerely,

Stephanie Shepard (signature)

Stephanie Shepard
804 N. Victoria Park Road
Ft. Myers, FL 30013
(813) 555-2000
(813) 555-5555

Now your job is complete. You can let your cover letter and résumé do the rest and land you the interview that very well could lead to the job you are seeking. (See also Appendix B.)

OBTAINING AN INTERVIEW

The interview is the focal point of the job search process. It is a meeting of a prospective employer and employee, and contrary to the thinking of many people, it is not a "one-way street." Interviewers are as anxious to find applicants meeting their employment standards as applicants are to obtain positions offering good experience and advancement possibilities.

This mutuality of interests requires complete frankness on the part of both the interviewer and the applicant. Employment arrangements predicated on false or erroneous representations are generally of short duration.

Naturally, employers want to know all about each applicant before offering him or her a position. They endeavor to assess during the course of an interview the applicant's interest, goals, technical background, college grades, college and community activities, personality, ability to use language grammatically and effectively, people skills, willingness and capacity to accept responsibility, and sense of loyalty. Sometimes testing devices are used as an aid in making selections, but more often employment decisions are made solely on the basis of personal reaction and the interviewer's evaluation.

Similarly, applicants want to know all about each prospective employer before reaching a decision concerning an employment offer. They inquire about the nature of the work, the location where they will be stationed, the extent of traveling involved, whether training programs are provided, if rapid advancement can be expected, and whether the prospective employer promotes from within the ranks, and whether promotion is based on merit or length of service. Applicants are justified in asking these and other pertinent questions in order to evaluate and compare both immediate and future possibilities with different employers.

The time allotted for interviewing each student on college campuses is usually thirty minutes. During this relatively short time, the above matters are discussed, and at least insofar as the employer is concerned, tentative employment decisions are made. Employers do not customarily make offers to students at the time of the campus interview, however. Those students considered good prospects are usually invited to visit one of the plants or offices of the employer at the employer's expense. Such visits provide an opportunity for employers to further evaluate students and for students to meet people with whom they might be working. After the office visit, the student is informed of the result, and when an offer is made, he or she is generally given several weeks to consider it before a reply is required.

Of course not all students or beginners can obtain positions through campus interviews, since only large organizations have college recruitment programs (even those seldom send recruiters to all colleges). For the many students and others who do not obtain positions through campus interviews, office interviews can be arranged by correspondence. June graduates should try to arrange for interviews several months before graduation. They will find that Christmas and spring vacations are excellent times to visit the offices of prospective employers; it is better to make definite appointments in advance. Thirty minutes to two hours or more are generally required for office interviews.

There is no fundamental difference between campus interviews and office interviews, except that final employment decisions are made by employers at office interviews. In each instance, the time element is important. The time allotted for interviews is relatively brief for an employer to size up an applicant and for an applicant to learn what an employer has to offer. Yet during this short period, applicants must be able to create a favorable impression. If they are unable to do so, they will find it difficult to obtain worthwhile positions. Therefore, applicants are well advised to find out as much as possible about prospective employers prior to being interviewed. If company literature is available, read it. General knowledge of a prospective employer's personnel practices, methods of operation, products sold or services performed, and the location of plants and offices will provide background for an applicant to ask intelligent questions during the interview. Knowledge of this kind generates self-confidence and helps create a favorable impression on interviewers.

An interview is more than a "talk fest." It starts from the moment the interviewer first sees the applicant. Poise, grace, appearance, and assurance can be identified at the time of introduction. The applicant's interest, which is an important factor, is determined by the general attitude evidenced, the questions asked, and the way they are asked. Careless or inappropriate dress, lack of poise and assurance, and inability to speak fluently, grammatically, and effectively are factors interviewers can most easily ascertain.

Applicants should be prepared to answer questions relating to college grades. It is noteworthy that in some fields, particularly accounting, employers generally place importance on grades as an indicator of potential. Consequently, applicants are frequently asked questions concerning their cumulative average in all subjects and in accounting subjects. Sometimes they are also asked to submit copies of their college records showing the marks received in each subject. Students and graduates can obtain copies of these records from their colleges. Those with good grades should be prepared to submit their college records to prospective employers during interviews.

While it is true that employers in the accounting field stress the importance of scholastic attainment, college grades are not necessarily the determining factor when making employment decisions. An applicant's personality and characteristics in relation to the position are equally important and often the deciding factors.

Employers expect applicants to "put their best foot forward." Accordingly, an applicant should not hesitate to explain a below-average scholastic record if there is justifiable reason for it. For example, if the overall grade point average stems from poor marks during the first two years followed by a notable improvement during the last two years, this should be pointed out. Similarly, if such grades are attributable to part-time work that interfered with time for study, this might be mentioned. Applicants should also mention scholastic attainments and extracurricular activities when these will bolster their applications. Such explanations, when tactfully made, have the added advantage of indicating ability to deal effectively with others. Obviously, if such explanations are presented the wrong way, they would be better left unsaid.

ADJUSTING TO THE NEW JOB

Getting started in a new job can be, and usually is, interesting, but for beginners with little or no business experience, it may not be easy. Difficulties encountered in getting started seldom stem from a lack of interest on the part of employers or uncooperativeness on the part of fellow employees but rather from the natural tensions that grow out of learning many new things in unfamiliar surroundings and making new associations within a short time.

A beginner may benefit from a formal orientation training program that gives insight into the employer's departmental organization and offers the new financial services employee an opportunity to meet a number of key personnel with whom he or she will later have dealings. But with or without such a program, trainees will have no difficulty during the initial employment period if they approach their jobs with earnestness, interest, and a willingness to learn.

Normally, the transition from school to the business world is uneventful and follows pretty much the pattern the beginner might anticipate from preemployment discussions with the employer. Sometimes, though, things may not work out as expected at the outset. Beginners may first be assigned to inconsequential or routine work, possibly quite unrelated to the positions for which they were employed. As a result, they may feel frustrated and discontented, especially if the importance of the new job was given a buildup at the time of hire. Such assignments may be of short duration, however, to fill in while arrangements are being completed for beginners to take up the responsibilities for which they were employed. Although considerate employers should explain this in advance, a wise beginner will accept such an assignment with good grace for a short time before seeking an explanation. The answer probably will become apparent without inquiry, and, in the meantime, nothing has been lost since any experience beginners receive adds to their general knowledge of the business. If the answer is not forthcoming within a reasonable time, in all fairness, the beginner should discuss this matter with the employer before seeking another position.

Obviously, new jobs require certain adjustments. For beginners who have had no previous full-time employment, the usual 9 A.M. to 5 P.M. office hours may seem somewhat long and confining, especially during the first few days when they have no fixed duties or responsibilities. This generally changes when their jobs take on meaning and they become better acquainted with other employees. During the first few days, beginners hesitate to ask questions, being unsure whether their questions concern things they are expected to know or if they will seem ignorant. Beginners might be compared with people who are given a jigsaw puzzle of a ship to assemble without being told if the ship is a sailing vessel, motor launch, or destroyer or whether it is ancient or modern. In these circumstances, matching the first few pieces causes difficulty, but as more pieces are assembled, the job gradually becomes easier and more interesting.

During the early stages of employment, beginners are observed critically. The manner in which they approach their work and deal with other employees is quickly noted. An attitude that can be described as "I've done my part by reporting for work; now it's up to you to teach me" is the best possible way to alienate employers and coworkers. On the other hand, those taking up their duties with interest and enthusiasm will find that they are credited for doing well and excused for their weaknesses. Of course, this does not go on forever; soon they are expected to do things right and take full responsibility for errors. They are instinctively catalogued by employers as good, average, or poor, and once so classified it becomes increasingly difficult to change first impressions.

APPENDIX

A

SELECTED PROFESSIONAL ASSOCIATIONS

The Actuarial Foundation
475 North Martingale Road, Suite 600
Schaumburg, IL 60173-2226
www.actuarialfoundation.org

American Academy of Actuaries
1100 Seventeenth Street, N.W., Seventh Floor
Washington, DC 20036
www.actuary.org

American Bankers Association
1120 Connecticut Avenue, N.W.
Washington, DC 20036
www.aba.com

American Institute for Chartered Property and Casualty
Underwriters/Insurance Institute of America
720 Providence Road
P.O. Box 3016
Malvern, PA 19355-0716
www.aicpcu.org

American Society of Pension Actuaries
4245 North Fairfax Drive, Suite 750
Arlington, VA 22203
www.aspa.org

Association for Computing Machinery (ACM)
1515 Broadway
New York, NY 10036
www.acm.org

Association for Information Systems
P.O. Box 2712
Atlanta, GA 30301-2712
www.aisnet.org

Association of Information Technology Professionals
401 North Michigan Avenue, Suite 2400
Chicago, IL 60611-4267
www.aitp.org

Association for Investment Management and Research
P.O. Box 3668
560 Ray C. Hunt Drive
Charlottesville, VA 22903-0668
www.aimr.com

Canadian Bankers Association
Box 348
Commerce Court West
199 Bay Street, 30th Floor
Toronto, Ontario
M5L 1G2 Canada
www.cba.ca

Canadian Institute of Actuaries (CIA)
150, rue Metcalfe Street, Suite/Bureau 800
Ottawa, Ontario
K2P 1P1 Canada
www.actuaries.ca

Consumer Bankers Association
1000 Wilson Boulevard, Suite 2500
Arlington, VA 22209-3912
www.cbanet.org

Credit Union National Association
P.O. Box 431
Madison, WI 53701
www.cna.org

Financial Executives International
200 Campus Drive
P.O. Box 674
Florham Park, NJ 07932
www.fei.org

Financial Planning Association
3801 East Florida Avenue, Suite 708
Denver, CO 80210
www.fpanet.org

Financial Women's Association of New York
215 Park Avenue South, Suite 1713
New York, NY 10003
www.fwa.org

Government Finance Officers Association
203 North LaSalle Street, Suite 2700
Chicago, IL 60601-1210
or
1301 Pennsylvania Avenue, N.W., Suite 309
Washington, D.C. 20004
www.gfoa.org

Health Insurance Association of America
555 13th Street, N.W., Suite 600 East
Washington, DC, 20004
www.hiaa.org

IEEE Computer Society
1730 Massachusetts Avenue, N.W.
Washington, DC 20036-1992
www.computer.org

Independent Community Bankers of America
One Thomas Circle N.W., Suite 400
Washington, DC 20005-5802
www.ibaa.org

International City/County Management Association
777 North Capitol Street, NE, Suite 500
Washington, DC 20002
www2.icma.org

Independent Automotive Damage Appraisers Association
P.O. Box 1166
Nixa, MO 65714
www.iada.org

Independent Insurance Agents of America
127 South Peyton Street
Alexandria, VA 22314
www.iiaa.org

Institute for Certification of Computing Professionals (ICCP)
2350 East Devon Avenue, Suite 115
Des Plaines, IL 60018
www.iccp.org

Institute of Management Accountants
10 Paragon Drive
Montvale, NJ 07645
www.imanet.org

Insurance Information Institute
110 William Street
New York, NY 10038
www.iii.org

Insurance Institute of America
720 Providence Road
P.O. Box 3016
Malvern, PA 19355-0716
www.aicpcu.org

International Institute of Municipal Clerks
1212 North San Dimas Canyon Road
San Dimas, CA 91773
www.iimc.com

International Claim Association
1255 23rd Street, N.W.
Washington, DC 20037
www.claim.org

Life Office Management Association
2300 Windy Ridge Parkway, Suite 600
Atlanta, GA 30339
www.loma.org

National Association of Health Underwriters
2000 North 14th Street, Suite 450
Arlington, VA 22201
www.nahu.org

New York Stock Exchange, Inc.
11 Wall Street
New York, NY 10005
www.nyse.com

Securities Industry Association
New York Office
120 Broadway, 35th Floor
New York, NY 10271-0080
www.sia.com

Securities Industry Association
Washington Office
1425 K Street, N.W., 7th Floor
Washington, DC 20005-3500
www.sia.com

APPENDIX

B

FURTHER READING IN CAREER PLANNING

Adams, Bob, and Laura Morin. *The Complete Résumé & Job Search Book for College Students*. 2nd ed. Avon, MA: Adams Media Corporation, 1999.

Bloch, Deborah Perlmutter. *How to Get Your First Job and Keep It*. 2nd ed. Chicago: VGM Career Books, 2002.

Bolles, Richard Nelson. *What Color Is Your Parachute 2004: A Practical Manual for Job-Hunters and Career Changers*. Berkeley, CA: Ten Speed Press, 2003.

Cunningham, John R. *The Inside Scoop: Recruiters Share Their Tips on Job Search Success with College Students*. New York: McGraw-Hill, 2001.

Deluca, Matthew J. *Best Answers to the 201 Most Frequently Asked Interview Questions*. New York: McGraw-Hill, 1996.

Deluca, Matthew, and Nanette Deluca. *More Best Answers to the 201 Most Frequently Asked Interview Questions*. New York: McGraw-Hill, 2001.

Drake, John D. *The Perfect Interview: How to Get the Job You Really Want*. 2nd ed. New York: AMACOM, American Management Association 2002.

Ebert, Marjorie, editor. *Résumés for First-Time Job Hunters*. Chicago: VGM Career Books, 2000.

Eisenberg, Ronni, and Kate Kelly. *Organize Your Job Search!* Boston, MA: Hyperion Press, 2000.

Gale, Linda, and Barry Gale. *Discover What You're Best At: A Complete Career System That Lets You Test Yourself to Discover Your Own True Career Abilities*. New York: Simon and Schuster, 1998.

Garber, Janet. *Getting a Job: An Easy, Smart Guide to Getting the Right Job*. New York: Silver Lining Books, 2003.

Gisler, Margaret, and Jamie Miller. *101 Career Alternatives for Teachers: Exciting Job Opportunities for Teachers Outside the Teaching Profession*. New York: Three Rivers Press, 2002.

Graber, Steven, and Barry Littmann. *Everything Online Job Search Book: Find the Jobs, Send Your Résumé, and Land the Career of Your Dreams—All Online!* Avon, MA: Adams Media Corporation, 2000.

Greene, Susan D., and Melanie C. Martel. *The Ultimate Job Hunter's Guidebook*. New York: Houghton Mifflin Company, 2000.

Griffiths, Bob. *Do What You Love for the Rest of Your Life: A Practical Guide to Career Change and Personal Renewal*. New York: Random House, 2001.

Jansen, Julie. *I Don't Know What I Want, but I Know It's Not This: A Step-By-Step Guide to Finding Gratifying Work*. New York: Penguin USA, 2003.

Masi, Mary, and Lauren B. Starkey. *Firefighter Career Starter*. Ayer, MA: Learning Express, 2001.

McKinney, Anne, editor. *Real Résumés for Career Changers: Actual Résumés and Cover Letters*. Fayetteville, NC: PREP Publishing, 2000.

O'Neill, Lucy. *Job Smarts*. New York: Scholastic Library Publishing, 2001.

Shar, Barbara, and Barbara Smith. *I Could Do Anything If I Only Knew What It Was: How to Discover What You Really Want and How to Get It*. New York: Dell Publishing, 1995.

Tieger, Paul, and Barbara Barron-Tieger. *Do What You Are: Discover the Perfect Career for You Through the Secrets of Personality Type*. Boston: Little, Brown and Company, 2001.

Whitcomb, Susan Britton, and Pat Kendall. *e-Résumés: Everything You Need to Know About Using Electronic Résumés to Tap into Today's Hot Job Market*. New York: McGraw-Hill, 2001.

APPENDIX

C

SELECTED UNIVERSITIES AND COLLEGES

Following is a state-by-state listing of selected colleges and universities that offer finance and banking courses. Each entry includes the school's address and website.

Other institutions also offer courses in these or related areas; check with a given school's catalog, website, or printed course schedule to learn more. Don't overlook your local community college if you are interested in programs offered at the two-year, associate degree level.

Alabama

Auburn University
202 Mary Martin Hall
Auburn, AL 36849
www.auburn.edu

Auburn University, Montgomery
Montgomery, AL 36117
www.aum.edu

Huntingdon College
1500 East Fairview Avenue
Montgomery, AL 36106
www.huntingdon.edu

Jacksonville State University
700 Pelham Road
Jacksonville, AL 36265
www.jsu.edu

Talladega College
627 West Battle Street
Talladega, AL 35160
www.talladega.edu

Tuskegee University
Tuskegee, AL 36088
www.tuskegee.edu

University of Alabama
P.O. Box 870132
Tuscaloosa, AL 35487
www.ua.edu

University of Alabama, Birmingham
UAB Station
1530 Third Avenue South
Birmingham, AL 35294
www.uab.edu

University of Alabama, Huntsville
University Center 119
Huntsville, AL 35899
www.uah.edu

University of South Alabama
Mobile, AL 36688
www.usouthal.edu

Alaska

University of Alaska, Anchorage
3211 Providence Drive
Anchorage, AK 99508
www.uaf.edu

University of Alaska, Fairbanks
P.O. Box 757480
Fairbanks, AK 99775
www.uaf.edu

Arizona

Arizona State University
University Drive and Mill Avenue
Tempe, AZ 85287
www.asu.edu

University of Arizona
P.O. Box 210108
Tucson, AZ 85721
www.arizona.edu

Western International University
9215 North Black Canyon Highway
Phoenix, AZ 85021
www.western.edu

Arkansas

Arkansas State University
P.O. Box 970
State University, AR 72467
www.astate.edu

Harding University
900 East Center
Searcy, AR 72149
www.harding.edu

Ouachita Baptist University
410 Ouachita Street
Arkadelphia, AR 71998
www.obu.edu

University of Arkansas at Little Rock
2801 South University Avenue
Little Rock, AR 72204
www.ualr.edu

University of Central Arkansas
201 Donaghey Avenue
Conway, AR 72035
www.uca.edu

California

California Baptist University
8432 Magnolia Avenue
Riverside, CA 92504
www.calbaptist.edu

California State Polytechnic University, Pomona
3801 West Temple Avenue
Pomona, CA 91768
www.csupomona.edu

California State University, Bakersfield
9001 Stockdale Highway
Bakersfield, CA 93311
www.csub.edu

California State University, Chico
400 West First Street
Chico, CA 95929
www.csuchico.edu

California State University, Fresno
5241 North Maple Avenue
Fresno, CA 93740
www.csufresno.edu

California State University, Fullerton
P.O. Box 6848
Fullerton, CA 92834
www.fullerton.edu

California State University, Hayward
25800 Carlos Bee Boulevard
Hayward, CA 94542
www.csuhayward.edu

California State University, Long Beach
1250 Bellflower Boulevard
Long Beach, CA 90840
www.csulb.edu

California State University, Los Angeles
5151 State University Drive
Los Angeles, CA 90032
www.calstatela.edu

California State University, Sacramento
6000 J Street
Sacramento, CA 95819
www.csus.edu

California State University, Stanislaus
810 West Monte Vista Avenue
Turlock, CA 95382
www.cssustan.edu

Chapman University
One Unity Drive
Orange, CA 92666
www.chapman.edu

Golden Gate University
536 Mission Street
San Francisco, CA 94105
www.gsu.edu

National University
11255 North Torrey Pines Road
La Jolla, CA 92037
www.nu.edu

San Diego State University
5300 Campanile Drive
San Diego, CA 92182
www.sdsu.edu

San Francisco State University
1600 Holloway Avenue
San Francisco, CA 94132
www.sfsu.edu

Santa Clara University
500 El Camino Real
Santa Clara, CA 95053
www.scu.edu

Stanford University
Stanford, CA 94305
www.stanford.edu

University of California, Berkeley
Haas School of Business
Berkeley, CA 94720
www.berkeley.edu

University of the Pacific
3601 Pacific Avenue
Stockton, CA 95211
www.uop.edu

University of Southern California
University Park
Los Angeles, CA 90089
www.usc.edu

Colorado

Adams State College
208 Edgemont Boulevard
Alamosa, CO 81102
www.adams.edu

Colorado State University
Fort Collins, CO 80523
www.colostate.edu

Mesa State College
P.O. Box 2647
Grand Junction, CO 81502
www.mesastate.edu

University of Colorado, Boulder
Leeds School of Business
Boulder, CO 80309
www.colorado.edu

University of Colorado, Colorado Springs
1420 Austin Bluffs Parkway
Colorado Springs, CO 80918
www.uccs.edu

University of Colorado, Denver
Auraria Campus
Denver, CO 80217
www.cudenver.edu

University of Denver
2101 South University Boulevard
Denver, CO 80208
www.du.edu

University of Northern Colorado
Greeley, CO 80639
www.unco.edu

Connecticut

Albertus Magnus College
700 Prospect Street
New Haven, CT 06511
www.albertus.edu

Eastern Connecticut State University
83 Windham Street
Hurley Hall
Willimantic, CT 06226
www.ecsu.edu

Fairfield University
1073 North Benson Road
Fairfield, CT 06824
www.fairfield.edu

Quinnipiac College
275 Mount Carmel Avenue
Hamden, CT 06518
www.quinnipiac.edu

University of Connecticut
2100 Hillside Road
Storrs, CT 06269
www.uconn.edu

University of Hartford
Barney School of Business
200 Bloomfield Avenue
West Hartford, CT 06117
www.hartford.edu

Delaware

Goldey-Beacon College
4701 Limestone Road
Wilmington, DE 19808
www.goldey.gbc.edu

University of Delaware
Alfred Lerner College of Business & Economics
Newark, DE 19716
www.udel.edu

District of Columbia

American University
4400 Massachusetts Avenue, N.W.
Kogod School of Business
Washington, DC 20016
www.american.edu

The George Washington University
2121 Eye Street, N.W.
Washington, DC 20052
www.gwu.edu

Georgetown University
37th and O Streets, N.W.
Washington, DC 200527
www.georgetown.edu

Howard University
2600 Sixth Street, N.W.
Washington, DC 20059
www.howard.edu

Florida

Barry University
Andreas School of Business
17300 North East Second Avenue
Miami Shores, FL 33161
www.barry.edu

Florida Atlantic University
777 Glades Boulevard
P.O. Box 3091
Boca Raton, FL 33431
www.fau.edu

Florida International University
11200 South West 8th Streeet
Miami, FL 33199
www.fiu.edu

Florida State University
Tallahassee, FL 32306
www.fsu.edu

Palm Beach Atlantic College
P.O. Box 24708
West Palm Beach, FL 33416
www.pbac.edu

Stetson University
421 North Woodland Boulevard
DeLand, FL 32723
www.stetson.edu

University of Central Florida
4000 Central Florida Boulevard
Orlando, FL 32816
www.ucf.edu

University of Florida
P.O. Box 117150
Gainesville, FL 32611
www.ufl.edu

University of Miami
School of Business
Coral Gables, FL 33124
www.miami.edu

University of North Florida
Goggin College of Business
4567 St. Johns Bluff Road
Jacksonville, FL 32224
www.unf.edu

University of South Florida
College of Business Administration
4203 East Fowler Avenue
Tampa, FL 33620
www.usf.edu

University of Tampa
John H. Sykes College of Business
401 East Fowler Avenue
Tampa, FL 33606
www.ut.edu

Georgia

Augusta State University
2500 Walton Way
Augusta, GA 30904
www.aug.edu

Berry College
2277 Martha Berry Highway, N.W.
Mount Berry, GA 30149
www.berry.edu

Clark Atlanta University
JP Brawley Drive, SW
Atlanta, GA 30314
www.cau.edu

Emory University
Atlanta, GA 30322
www.emory.edu

Georgia Southern University
U.S. 301 South
Statesboro, GA 30460
www.georgiasouthern.edu

Georgia State University
Robinson College of Business
33 Gilmer Street, S.E.
Atlanta, GA 30303
www.gsu.edu

Kennesaw State University
Michael J. Coles College of Business
1000 Chastain Road
Kennesaw, GA 30144
www.kennesaw.edu

Morehouse College
830 Westview Drive, SW
Atlanta, GA 30314
www.morehouse.edu

State University of West Georgia
1600 Maple Street
Carrollton, GA 30118
www.westga.edu

University of Georgia
Terry College of Business
Athens, GA 30602
www.uga.edu

Hawaii

Hawaii Pacific University
1164 Bishop Street
Honolulu, HI 96813
www.hpu.edu

University of Hawaii, Manoa
2404 Maile Way
Honolulu, HI 96822
www.hawaii.edu

Idaho

Boise State University
1910 University Drive
Boise, ID 83725
www.boisestate.edu

Idaho State University
College of Business
921 South 8th Avenue
Pocatello, ID 83209
www.isu.edu

University of Idaho
Moscow, ID 83844
www.uidaho.edu

Illinois

Bradley University
Foster College of Business
1501 West Bradley Avenue
Peoria, IL 61625
www.bradley.edu

Chicago State University
95th Street at King Drive
Chicago, IL 60628
www.csu.edu

DePaul University
1 East Jackson Boulevard
Chicago, IL 60604
www.depaul.edu

Eastern Illinois University
600 Lincoln Avenue
Charleston, IL 61920
www.eui.edu

Illinois State University
Normal, IL 61790
www.ilstu.edu

Loyola University of Chicago
25 East Pearson
Chicago, IL 60611
www.luc.edu

Northern Illinois University
P.O. Box 3001
DeKalb, IL 60115
www.niu.edu

Olivet Nazarene University
P.O. Box 527
Kankakee, IL 60901
www.olivet.edu

Rockford College
5050 East State Street
Rockford, IL 61108
www.rockford.edu

Roosevelt University
430 South Michigan Avenue
Chicago, IL 60605
www.roosevelt.edu

Southern Illinois University, Carbondale
Carbondale, IL 62901
www.siu.edu

University of Illinois, Chicago
601 South Morgan
Chicago, IL 60680
www.uic.edu

University of Illinois, Urbana-Champaign
1401 West Green Street
Urbana, IL 61801
www.uiuc.edu

Western Illinois University
College of Business and Technology
1 University Circle
Macomb, IL 61455
www.wiu.edu

Indiana
Ball State University
WB 100
Muncie, IN 47306
www.bsu.edu

Butler University
4600 Sunset Avenue
Indianapolis, IN 46208
www.butler.edu

Franklin College of Indiana
501 East Monroe Street
Franklin, IN 46131
www.franklincoll.edu

Indiana State University
School of Business
Terre Haute, IN 47809
www.indstate.edu

Indiana University, Bloomington
1309 East Tenth Street
Bloomington, IN 47405
www.iub.edu

Indiana University–Purdue University, Fort Wayne
2101 Coliseum Boulevard East
Fort Wayne, IN 46805
www.ipfw.edu

Marian College
5200 Cold Spring Road
Indianapolis, IN 46222
www.marian.edu

Purdue University
Schleman Hall
West Lafayette, IN 47907
www.purdue.edu

Saint Mary's College
Notre Dame, IN 46556
www.saintmarys.edu

University of Notre Dame
Notre Dame, IN 46556
www.nd.edu

University of Southern Indiana
8600 University Boulevard
Evansville, IN 47712
www.usi.edu

Valparaiso University
Valparaiso, IN 46383
www.valpo.edu

Iowa

Drake University
2507 University Avenue
Des Moines, IA 50311
www.drake.edu

Grand View College
1200 Grandview Avenue
Des Moines, IA 50316
www.gvc.edu

Iowa State University
Ames, IA 50011
www.iastate.edu

University of Iowa
Henry B. Tippie College of Business
Iowa City, IA 52242
www.uiowa.edu

University of Northern Iowa
College of Business Administration
120 Gilchrist Hall
Cedar Falls, IA 50614
www.uni.edu

Kansas

Benedictine College
1020 North 2nd Street
Atchison, KS 66002
www.benedictine.edu

Emporia State University
1200 Commercial Street
Emporia, KS 66801
www.emporia.edu

Kansas State University
Manhattan, KS 66506
www.k-state.edu

McPherson College
1600 East Euclid
McPherson, KS 67460
www.mcpherson.edu

Pittsburg State University
1701 South Broadway
Pittsburg, KS 66762
www.pittstate.edu

Wichita State University
Barton School of Business
1845 North Fairmount
Wichita, KS 67260
www.wichita.edu

Kentucky

Eastern Kentucky University
521 Lancaster Avenue
Richmond, KY 40475
www.eku.edu

Georgetown College
400 East College Street
Georgetown, KY 40324
www.georgetowncollege.edu

Murray State University
P.O. Box 9
Murray, KY 42071
www.murraystate.edu

Northern Kentucky University
BEP 401, Nunn Drive
Highland Heights, KY 41099
www.nku.edu

University of Kentucky
Lexington, KY 40506
www.uky.edu

University of Louisville
2301 South Third Street
Louisville, KY 40292
www.louisville.edu

Western Kentucky University
Gordon Ford College of Business
1 Big Red Way
Bowling Green, KY 42101
www.wku.edu

Louisiana

Grambling State University
100 Main Street
Grambling, LA 71245
www.gram.edu

Louisiana College
P.O. Box 560
Pineville, LA 71359
www.lacollege.edu

Louisiana State University, Shreveport
One University Place
Shreveport, LA 71115
www.lsus.edu

Louisiana Tech University
Box 10318
Ruston, LA 71272
www.latech.edu

Loyola University
6363 Saint Charles Avenue
New Orleans, LA 70118
www.loyno.edu

McNeese State University
4205 Ryan Street
Lake Charles, LA 70609
www.mcneece.edu

Nicholls State University
P.O. Box 2015
Thibodaux, LA 70310
www.nicholls.edu

Southeastern Louisiana University
SLU Box 10735
Hammond, LA 70402
www.selu.edu

Tulane University
6823 St. Charles Avenue
New Orleans, LA 70118
www.tulane.edu

University of New Orleans
2000 Lakeshore Drive
New Orleans, LA 70148
www.uno.edu

Maine

Husson College
One College Circle
Bangor, ME 04401
www.husson.edu

Thomas College
180 West River Road
Waterville, ME 04901
www.thomas.edu

University of Maine
Orono, ME 04469
www.umaine.edu

Maryland

Morgan State University
1700 East Cold Spring Lane
Baltimore, MD 21251
www.morgan.edu

Towson State University
800 York Road
Baltimore, MD 21252
www.towson.edu

University of Baltimore
Merrick School of Business
Baltimore, MD 21201
www.ubalt.edu

University of Maryland, College Park
College Park, MD 20742
www.umd.edu

Massachusetts

Babson College
231 Forest Street
Babson Park, MA 02457
www.babson.edu

Bentley College
175 Forest Street
Waltham, MA 02452
www.bentley.edu

Boston College
140 Commonwealth Avenue
Chestnut Hill, MA 02467
www.bc.edu

Boston University
595 Commonwealth Avenue
Boston, MA 02215
www.bu.edu

Harvard University
Cambridge, MA 02138
www.harvard.edu

Merrimack College
315 Turnpike Road
North Andover, MA 01845
www.merrimack.edu

Northeastern University
360 Huntington Avenue
Boston, MA 02115
www.neu.edu

Salem State College
352 Lafayette Street
Salem, MA 01970
www.salemstate.edu

Suffolk University
8 Ashburton Place
Boston, MA 02108
www.suffolk.edu

University of Massachusetts, Amherst
Amherst, MA 01003
www.umass.edu

University of Massachusetts, Dartmouth
285 Old Westport Road
North Dartmouth, MA 02747
www.umassd.edu

University of Massachusetts, Lowell
One University Avenue
Lowell, MA 01854
www.uml.edu

Western New England College
1215 Wilbraham Road
Springfield, MA 01119
www.wnec.edu

Michigan

Alma College
614 West Superior Street
Alma, MI 48801
www.alma.edu

Central Michigan University
Mount Pleasant, MI 48859
www.cmich.edu

Eastern Michigan University
College of Business
Ypsilanti, MI 48197
www.emich.edu

Grand Valley State University
1 College Drive
Allendale, MI 49401
www.gvsu.edu

Hillsdale College
33 East College
Hillsdale, MI 49242
www.hillsdale.edu

Madonna University
36600 Schoolcraft Road
Livonia, MI 48150
www.madonna.edu

Michigan State University
Eli Broad College of Business
East Lansing, MI 48824
www.msu.edu

Michigan Technological University
1400 Townsend Drive
Houghton, MI 49931
www.mtu.edu

Northern Michigan University
1401 Presque Isle Avenue
Marquette, MI 49855
www.nmu.edu

Oakland University
Rochester, MI 48309
www.oakland.edu

Olivet College
320 South Main Street
Olivet, MI 49076
www.olivetcollege.edu

Saginaw Valley State College
7400 Bay Road
University Center, MI 48710
www.svsu.edu

University of Michigan, Ann Arbor
Ann Arbor, MI 48109
www.umich.edu

University of Michigan, Dearborn
4901 Evergreen Road
Dearborn, MI 48128
www.umd.umich.edu

University of Michigan, Flint
245 University Pavilion
Flint, MI 48502
www.umflint.edu

Wayne State University
Detroit, MI 48202
www.wayne.edu

Western Michigan University
Haworth College of Business
Kalamazoo, MI 49008
www.wmich.edu

Minnesota

Minnesota State University
MH120
Mankato, MN 56001
www.mnsu.edu

St. Cloud State University
720 Fourth Avenue South
Saint Cloud, MN 56301
www.stcloudstate.edu

University of Minnesota, Duluth
Labovitz School of Business & Economics
1049 University Drive
Duluth, MN 55812
www.d.umn.edu

Mississippi

Delta State University
Cleveland, MS 38733
www.deltastate.edu

Mississippi State University
P.O. Box 5288
Mississippi State, MS 39762
www.msstate.edu

University of Mississippi
University, MS 38677
www.olemiss.edu

University of Southern Mississippi
11 College Drive
Hattiesburg, MS 39406
www.usm.edu

Missouri

Avila College
11901 Wornall Road
Kansas City, MO 64145
www.avila.edu

Central Missouri State University
P.O. Box 800
Warrensburg, MO 64093
www.cmsu.edu

Fontbonne College
6800 Wydown Boulevard
St. Louis, MO 63105
www.fontbonne.edu

Lindenwood University
205 South Kings Highway
St. Charles, MO 63301
www.lindenwood.edu

Northwest Missouri State University
800 University Drive
Maryville, MO 64468
www.nwmissouri.edu

Saint Louis University
221 North Grand Boulevard
St. Louis, MO 63103
www.slu.edu

Southeast Missouri State University
One University Plaza
Cape Girardeau, MO 63701
www.semo.edu

Southwest Missouri State University
901 South National Avenue
Springfield, MO 65804
www.smsu.edu

Truman State University
205 McClain Hall
Kirksville, MO 63501
www.truman.edu

University of Missouri, Columbia
219 Jesse Hall
Columbia, MO 65211
www.missouri.edu

Washington University
Campus Box 1133
St. Louis, MO 63130
www.wustl.edu

Montana

Carroll College
1601 North Benton Avenue
Helena, MT 59625
www.carroll.edu

Montana State University, Bozeman
120 Hamilton Hall
Bozeman, MT 59717
www.montana.edu

Montana Tech of the University of Montana
1300 West Park Street
Butte, MT 59701
www.mtech.edu

University of Montana
32 Campus Drive
Missoula, MT 59812
www.umt.edu

Nebraska

Creighton University
2500 California Plaza
Omaha, NE 68178
www.creighton.edu

Dana College
2848 College Drive
Blair, NE 68008
www.dana.edu

University of Nebraska, Lincoln
Lincoln, NE 68588
www.unl.edu

University of Nebraska, Omaha
6001 Dodge Street
Omaha, NE 68182
www.unomaha.edu

Nevada

University of Nevada, Las Vegas
4505 Maryland Parkway
Las Vegas, NV 89154
www.unlv.edu

University of Nevada, Reno
1664 North Virginia Street
Reno, NV 89557
www.unr.edu

New Hampshire

Franklin Pierce College
20 College Road
Rindge, NH 03461
www.fpc.edu

University of New Hampshire
Whittemore School of Business and Economics
15 College Road
Durham, NH 03824
www.unh.edu

New Jersey

College of New Jersey
2000 Pennington Road
Ewing, NJ 08628
www.tcnj.edu

Fairleigh Dickinson University
1000 River Road
Teaneck, NJ 07666
www.fde.edu

Monmouth University
West Long Branch, NJ 07764
www.monmouth.edu

Montclair State University
Upper Montclair, NJ 07043
www.montclair.edu

Ramapo College of New Jersey
505 Ramapo Valley Road
Mahwah, NJ 07430
www.ramapo.edu

Rider University
2083 Lawrenceville Road
Lawrenceville, NJ 08648
www.rider.edu

Rowan University
201 Mullica Hill Road
Glassboro, NJ 08028
www.rowan.edu

Rutgers University, State University of New Jersey
New Brunswick, NJ 08903
www.rutgers.edu

Seton Hall University
400 South Orange Avenue
South Orange, NJ 07079
www.shu.edu

New Mexico

Eastern New Mexico University
1200 West University
Portales, NM 88130
www.enmu.edu

New Mexico State University
Box 30001
Las Cruces, NM 88003
www.nmsu.edu

New York

Adelphi University
Garden City, NY 11530
www.adelphi.edu

Alfred University
One Saxon Drive
Alfred, NY 14802
www.alfred.edu

Canisius College
2001 Main Street
Buffalo, NY 14208
www.canisius.edu

City University of New York, Baruch College
One Baruch Way
New York, NY 10010
www.baruch.cuny.edu

Clarkson University
Potsdam, NY 13699
www.clarkson.edu

Dominican College
470 Western Highway
Orangeburg, NY 10962
www.dominican.edu

Fordham University
Rose Hill Campus
Bronx, NY 10458
www.fordham.edu

Hofstra University
Hempstead, NY 11549
www.hofstra.edu

Iona College
715 North Avenue
New Rochelle, NY 10801
www.iona.edu

Long Island University, C.W. Post Campus
720 Post Campus
Brookville, NY 11548
www.cwpost.liu.edu

Manhattan College
Manhattan College Parkway
Riverdale, NY 10471
www.manhattan.edu

Manhattanville College
2900 Purchase Street
Purchase, NY 10577
www.mville.edu

New York University
22 Washington Square North
44 West Fourth Street
New York, NY 10012
www.nyu.edu

Pace University
1 Pace Plaza
New York, NY 10038
www.pace.edu

Rensselaer Polytechnic Institute
110 8th Street
Troy, NY 12180
www.rpi.edu

Rochester Institute of Technology
One Lomb Memorial Drive
Rochester, NY 14623
www.rit.edu

St. John Fisher College
3690 East Avenue
Rochester, NY 14618
www.sfjc.edu

Saint John's University
800 Utopia Parkway
Jamaica, NY 11439
www.stjohns.edu

State University of New York, Brockport
350 New Campus Drive
Brockport, NY 14420
www.brockport.edu

Syracuse University
201 Tolley Administration Building
Syracuse, NY 13244
www.syracuse.edu

North Carolina

Appalachian State University
Boone, NC 28608
www.appstate.edu

Duke University
Fuqua School of Business
Durham, NC 27708
www.duke.edu

East Carolina University
East Fifth Street
Greenville, NC 27858
www.ecu.edu

Mars Hill College
100 Athletic Street
Mars Hill, NC 28754
www.mhc.edu

University of North Carolina, Charlotte
9201 University City Boulevard
Charlotte, NC 28223
www.uncc.edu

University of North Carolina, Greensboro
P.O. Box 26165
Greensboro, NC 27412
www.uncg.edu

University of North Carolina, Wilmington
601 South College Road
Wilmington, NC 28403
www.uncw.edu

Western Carolina University
Cullowhee, NC 28723
www.uncw.edu

North Dakota

Dickinson State University
291 Campus Drive
Dickinson, ND 58601
www.dsu.nodak.edu

University of North Dakota
University Station
College of Business and Public Administration
P.O. Box 7144
Grand Forks, ND 58202
www.und.edu

Ohio

Ashland University
401 College Avenue
Ashland, OH 44805
www.ashland.edu

Bowling Green State University
College of Business Administration
Bowling Green, OH 43403
www.bgsu.edu

Case Western Reserve University
Cleveland, OH 44106
www.cwru.edu

Cedarville College
Box 601
Cedarville, OH 45314
www.cedarville.edu

Cleveland State University
1860 East 18th Avenue
Cleveland, OH 44114
www.csuohio.edu

Defiance College
701 North Clinton Street
Defiance, OH 43512
www.defiance.edu

John Carroll University
20700 North Park Boulevard
University Heights, OH 44118
www.jcu.edu

Kent State University
P.O. Box 5190
Kent, OH 44242
www.kent.edu

Miami University
Oxford, OH 45056
www.muohio.edu

Ohio Northern University
525 South Main Street
Ada, OH 45810
www.onu.edu

Ohio State University
Fisher College of Business
Columbus, OH 43210
www.osu.edu

Ohio University
Chubb Hall 120
Athens, OH 45701
www.ohiou.edu

University of Akron
259 South Broadway
Akron, OH 44325
www.uakron.edu

University of Dayton
300 College Park
Dayton, OH 45469
www.dayton.edu

University of Toledo
Toledo, OH 43606
www.utoledo.edu

Wright State University
3460 Colonel Glenn Highway
Dayton, OH 45435
www.wright.edu

Xavier University
3800 Victory Parkway
Cincinnati, OH 45207
www.xu.edu

Youngstown State University
One University Plaza
Youngstown, OH 44555
www.ysu.edu

Oklahoma

East Central University
Ada, OK 74820
www.ecok.edu

Oklahoma Baptist University
500 West University
Shawnee, OK 74801
www.okbu.edu

Oklahoma State University
College of Business Administration
Stillwater, OK 74078
www.okstate.edu

University of Oklahoma
407 West Boyd
Norman, OK 73019
www.ou.edu

University of Tulsa
600 South College
Tulsa, OK 74104
www.utulsa.edu

Oregon

Oregon State University
200 Bexell
Corvallis, OR 97331
www.oregonstate.edu

Pacific University
2043 College Way
Forest Grove, OR 97116
www.pacificu.edu

Portland State University
P.O. Box 751
Portland, OR 97207
www.pdx.edu

University of Oregon
Eugene, OR 97403
www.uoregon.edu

University of Portland
5000 North Willamette Boulevard
Portland, OR 97203
www.up.edu

Pennsylvania

Cabrini College
610 King of Prussia Road
Radnor, PA 19087
www.cabrini.edu

Carnegie Mellon University
5000 Forbes Avenue
Pittsburgh, PA 15213
www.cmu.edu

Clarion University of Pennsylvania
Clarion, PA 16214
www.clarion.edu

Drexel University
5141 Chestnut Street
Philadelphia, PA 19104
www.drexel.edu

Grove City College
100 Campus Drive
Grove City, PA 16127
www.gcc.edu

Indiana University of Pennsylvania
664 Pratt Drive
Indiana, PA 15705
www.iup.edu

King's College
133 North River Street
Wilkes-Barre, PA 18711
www.kings.edu

LaSalle University
1900 West Olney Avenue
Philadelphia, PA 19141
www.lasalle.edu

Lehigh University
27 Memorial Drive West
Bethlehem, PA 18015
www.lehigh.edu

Pennsylvania State University
Smeal College of Business
University Park, PA 16802
www.psu.edu

Pennsylvania State University, Harrisburg
777 West Harrisburg Pike
Middletown, PA 17057
www.hbg.psu.cdu

Saint Joseph's University
5600 City Avenue
Philadelphia, PA 19131
www.sju.edu

Shippensburg University of Pennsylvania
1871 Old Main Drive
Shippensburg, PA 17257
www.ship.edu

Susquehanna University
Selinsgrove, PA 17870
www.susqu.edu

Temple University
Philadelphia, PA 19122
www.temple.edu

University of Pennsylvania
3451 Walnut Street
Philadelphia, PA 19104
www.upenn.edu

University of Pittsburgh
Pittsburgh, PA 15260
www.pitt.edu

University of Scranton
800 Linden Street
Scranton, PA 18510
www.scranton.edu

Rhode Island

Bryant College
1150 Douglas Pike
Smithfield, RI 02917
www.bryant.edu

Providence College
549 River Avenue
Providence, RI 02918
www.providence.edu

Salve Regina University
100 Ochre Point Avenue
Newport, RI 02840
www.salve.edu

University of Rhode Island
Kingston, RI 02881
www.uri.edu

South Carolina

Clemson University
165 Serrine Hall
Box 345124
Clemson, SC 29634
www.clemson.edu

Coker College
300 East College Avenue
Hartsville, SC 29550
www.coker.edu

Francis Marion University
P.O. Box 100547
Florence, SC 29501
www.fmarion.edu

University of South Carolina, Aiken
471 University Parkway
Aiken, SC 29801
www.sc.edu

Wofford College
429 North Church Street
Spartanburg, SC 29303
www.wofford.edu

South Dakota

Augustana College
2001 Summit Avenue
Sioux Falls, SD 57197
www.augie.edu

Dakota State University
820 North Washington Avenue
Madison, SD 57042
www.dsu.edu

University of South Dakota
Vermillion, SD 57069
www.usd.edu

Tennessee

Austin Peay State University
P.O. Box 4548
Clarksville, TN 37044
www.apsu.edu

East Tennessee State University
P.O. Box 70699
Johnson City, TN 37614
www.etsu.edu

Fisk University
1000 17th Avenue North
Nashville, TN 37208
www.fisk.edu

Middle Tennessee State University
Box 101
Murfreesboro, TN 37132
www.mtsu.edu

Tennessee Technological University
Box 5025
Cookeville, TN 38505
www.tntech.edu

University of Memphis
Fogelman College of Business & Economics
Memphis, TN 38152
www.memphis.edu

University of Tennessee, Chattanooga
615 McCallie Avenue
Chattanooga, TN 37403
www.utc.edu

University of Tennessee, Knoxville
Knoxville, TN 37996
www.utk.edu

University of Tennessee, Martin
544 University Street
Martin, TN 38238
www.utm.edu

Texas

Baylor University
P.O. Box 97056
Waco, TX 76798
www.baylor.edu

Dallas Baptist University
3000 Mountain Creek Parkway
Dallas, TX 75211
www.dbu.edu

Hardin-Simmons University
Box 16050
Abilene, TX 79698
www.hstx.edu

Lamar University
P.O. Box 10009
Beaumont, TX 77710
www.lamar.edu

McMurry University
Box 278
Abilene, TX 79697
www.mcm.edu

Saint Mary's University of San Antonio
One Camino Santa Maria
San Antonio, TX 78228
www.stmarytx.edu

Sam Houston State University
Huntsville, TX 77341
www.shsu.edu

Southern Methodist University
Box 296
Dallas, TX 75275
www.smu.edu

Stephen R. Austin State University
Box 13004
Nacogdoches, TX 75962
www.sfasu.edu

Texas A&M International University
5201 University Boulevard
Laredo, TX 78041
www.tamiu.edu

Texas A&M University
College Station, TX 77843
www.tamu.edu

Texas A&M University, Corpus Christi
6300 Ocean Drive
Corpus Christi, TX 78412
www.tamucc.edu

Texas Christian University
P.O. Box 298530
Forth Worth, TX 76129
www.tcu.edu

Texas Southern University
3100 Cleburne Street
Houston, TX 77004
www.tsu.edu

Texas Tech University
Rawls College of Business
2500 Broadway
Lubbock, TX 79409
www.ttu.edu

Texas Wesleyan University
1201 Wesleyan
Fort Worth, TX 76105
www.txwesleyan.edu

University of Texas, Arlington
701 South Nedderman Drive
Arlington, TX 76019
www.uta.edu

University of Texas, Austin
McCombs School of Business
1 University Station
Austin, TX 78712
www.utexas.edu

University of Texas, El Paso
500 West University Avenue
El Paso, TX 79968
www.utep.edu

University of Texas, Pan American
Edinburg, TX 78539
www.panam.edu

University of Texas, San Antonio
6900 North Loop 1604 West
San Antonio, TX 78249
www.utsa.edu

Utah

Brigham Young University
Provo, UT 84602
www.byu.edu

University of Utah
1645 East Campus Center Drive
Salt Lake City, UT 84112
www.utah.edu

Utah State University
Logan, UT 84322
www.usu.edu

Weber State University
3750 Harrison Boulevard
Ogden, UT 84408
www.weber.edu

Vermont

Green Mountain College
One College Circle
Poultney, VT 05764
www.greenmtn.edu

University of Vermont
55 Colchester Avenue
Burlington, VT 05405
www.uvm.edu

Virginia

George Mason University
4400 University Drive
Fairfax, VA 22030
www.gmu.edu

James Madison University
800 South Main Street
Harrisonburg, VA 22807
www.jmu.edu

Longwood University
201 High Street
Farmville, VA 23909
www.longwood.edu

Old Dominion University
2004 Constant Hall
Norfolk, VA 23529
www.odu.edu

Radford University
East Main Street
Radford, VA 24142
www.radford.edu

University of Richmond
1 Gateway Drive
Richmond, VA 23173
www.richmond.edu

Virginia Commonwealth University
Box 84400
Richmond, VA 23284
www.vcu.edu

Virginia Polytechnic Institute and State University
201 Burruss Hall
Blacksburg, VA 24061
www.vt.edu

Washington

Eastern Washington University
526 5th Street
Cheney, WA 99004
www.ewu.edu

Gonzaga University
502 East Boone Street
Spokane, WA 99258
www.gonzaga.edu

Pacific Lutheran University
Tacoma, WA 98447
www.pl.edu

Seattle University
900 Broadway
Seattle, WA 98122
www.seattle.edu

University of Washington
Box 353200
Seattle, WA 98195
www.washington.edu

Washington State University
P.O. Box 641067
Pullman, WA 99164
www.wsu.edu

Western Washington University
516 High Street
Bellingham, WA 98225
www.wwu.edu

West Virginia

Bethany College
Bethany, WV 26032
www.bethanywv.edu

Fairmont State College
1201 Locust Avenue
Fairmont, WV 26554
www.fscwv.edu

Marshall University
Lewis College of Business
Huntington, WV 25755
www.marshall.edu

West Liberty State College
P.O. Box 295
West Liberty, WV 26074
www.wlsc.edu

West Virginia University
Box 6025
Morgantown, WV 26506
www.wvu.edu

Wisconsin

Concordia University Wisconsin
12800 North Lake Shore Drive
Mequon, WI 53097
www.cuw.edu

Marquette University
P.O. Box 1881
Milwaukee, WI 53201
www.mu.edu

University of Wisconsin, Eau Claire
105 Garfield Avenue
Eau Claire, WI 54702
www.uwec.edu

University of Wisconsin, LaCrosse
1725 State Street
LaCrosse, WI 54601
www.uwlax.edu

University of Wisconsin, Madison
Madison, WI 53706
www.wisc.edu

University of Wisconsin, Milwaukee
P.O. Box 413
Milwaukee, WI 53201
www.uwm.edu

University of Wisconsin, Oshkosh
Oshkosh, WI 54901
www.uwosh.edu

University of Wisconsin, Parkside
900 Wood Road
Box 2000
Kenosha, WI 53141
www.uwp.edu

University of Wisconsin, Whitewater
800 West Main Street
Whitewater, WI 53190
www.uww.edu

Wyoming

University of Wyoming
1000 East University Avenue
Laramie, WY 82071
www.uwyo.edu

GLOSSARY

Acquisition One company taking over the controlling interest in another company.

Bank A financial institution that provides loans, savings and checking accounts, and various other financial services; sometimes the term *commercial bank* is used to differentiate this type of bank from an investment banking firm.

Bond A security through which the issuer borrows money from investors. The issuer, which may be a corporation or unit of government, promises to pay the bondholder the bond's face value, plus interest, over a specified period of time.

Broker A person or firm making securities trades for a fee or commission.

Controller The key financial executive who controls, analyzes, and interprets the financial results and records of a company or an organization (also spelled comptroller).

Convertible security A bond or preferred stock that may be exchanged for common stock or another security specified by the issuer.

Credit union A member-owned, not-for-profit financial institution that provides loans, savings accounts, and other services to its members.

Derivative security A financial instrument, such as a futures or options contract, whose value is related to the value of another security, known as the underlying security.

Dividend The share of corporate profits paid to stockholders.

Endowment A fund set up to provide a perpetual source of investment income for an institution, especially a college or university.

Entrepreneur A person who develops a business, assuming the risk for the sake of the profit.

Exchange A center where certain securities or commodities may be bought and sold. Instruments bought and sold there are said to be exchange listed or exchange traded.

Financial planning The act of advising individuals, or in some cases corporations, about not only how to manage their investments but how to best meet their other financial needs, such as buying insurance, financing children's education, or planning the distribution of estates.

Foundation A fund whose investment earnings are used to provide charitable donations.

Futures contract A promise to buy or sell a specified security or commodity, or group of securities or commodities, at a fixed point in the future.

Interest The charge paid for a loan by the borrower to the lender.

Investment banking The industry encompassing firms that underwrite securities and provide brokerage services.

Investment management (also called *portfolio management* or *asset management*) The process of choosing securities to be bought or sold for one's own account or that of a client.

Market The stock market; any market for stocks or bonds.

Merger The act or process of joining two or more companies into one company.

Mortgage A pledge of property, often a home, to a lender as security on a loan.

Options contract A promise to buy or sell a security or commodity, or group of securities or commodities, at a specified price within a specified time.

Over-the-counter A securities trade that does not take place on an exchange; the term *over-the-counter market* is also used to describe the computerized NASDAQ system that links people and firms making such trades.

Pension fund A fund set up by an employer to provide for present and future obligations to retirees. The fund generally is invested in a variety of financial instruments, such as stocks, bonds, real estate, and venture capital. Depending on the type of pension arrangement the employer offers, the return on the investments may or may not affect retiree benefits. In a defined benefit plan, retirees are promised a set monthly benefit no matter how the fund's investments perform. In a defined contribution plan, the payout, usually given as a lump sum on retirement, is determined by investment performance. Many employers allow workers a say in the investments of defined contribution plans.

Portfolio All the securities held for investment by an individual, bank, or company.

Stock A security entitling the holder to ownership of a share of a corporation. Companies may issue common stock and preferred stock. Holders of common stock generally have the right to vote on corporate management and policies; preferred stock usually carries no voting rights. Dividends paid on common stock may vary, but preferred stock has a fixed annual dividend. Preferred stock takes precedence over common stock for dividend payments and distribution of assets should the company be liquidated.

Trader A person employed by a financial institution who is responsible for giving brokers orders to buy or sell securities for the institution, or a person who makes those trades on the floor of a securities exchange. On a securities exchange, traders may negotiate on behalf of a brokerage firm and its clients or may use their own money to trade; the latter are said to be trading for their own accounts.

Underwriting The act, usually performed by an investment banking firm, of buying newly issued stocks or bonds from the issuer (a corporation or government entity) and reselling them to investors.

Venture capital The money provided by investors to a new or growing company whose stock is not yet publicly traded.

ABOUT THE AUTHOR

Trudy Ring has written about business and finance for newspapers, magazines, and reference books. She was a reporter for *Pensions & Investments* for six years, and her work also has appeared in *Global Finance, USA Today,* and the *International Directory of Company Histories*. Ms. Ring also writes about other subjects ranging from health to the arts.

Mark Rowh, who revised and updated the current edition, is the author of a number of books, including *Careers in Real Estate* and *Winning Government Grants and Contracts for Your Small Business*.